In Defence Of Plain English

Victoria Branden

In Defence of Plain English

The Decline and Fall of Literacy in Canada

HOUNSLOW

In Defence of Plain English
The Decline and Fall of Literacy in Canada

ISBN 0-88882-143-3

Publisher: Anthony Hawke
Editor: Shirley Knight Morris
Designer: Gerard Williams
Compositor: Robin Brass Studio
Printer: Best Gagné Book Manufacturers

Publication was assisted by the Canada Council, the
Ontario Arts Council and the Ontario Ministry of Culture
and Communications.

Hounslow Press
A Division of Anthony R. Hawke limited
124 Parkview Avenue
Willowdale, Ontario, Canada
M2N 3Y5

Printed and bound in Canada

This is for the Rycrofts –
Jan and Don and Ben and Jake

They play great hockey and never Talk Classy

Contents

Foreword

Long ago, in 1946, George Orwell observed that most people who thought about it at all admitted that the English language was in a bad way: "But it is generally assumed that we cannot by conscious action do anything about it."

I have begun to fear that it is not merely in a bad way, but that it is threatened with extinction, that we will lose the faculty altogether and be reduced to mere gibbering.

Orwell compared the malady afflicting English with alcoholism.

> A man may take to drink because he feels himself to be a failure, and then fail all the more completely because he drinks. It is rather the same thing that is happening to the English language. It becomes ugly and inaccurate because our thoughts are foolish, but the slovenliness of our language makes it easier . . . to have foolish thoughts.

His chief concerns were jargon, staleness of imagery, and lack of precision. Halcyon days, when those were our chief language problems! What would George think if he were alive today? Our poor old language has reached a state of such unexampled degradation that rescue may be hopeless. We have abused it as we have abused the environment, and have neglected the application of remedies until it may well be, in both cases, too late.

This unhappy state of affairs is usually blamed on the education system. "Lazy, permissive teachers are short-changing our children!" lectured no less an authority than the *National Enquirer* – and who can argue with that august publication? Nevertheless, children spend far more time sitting in front of the TV than listening to the teacher. (They may spend more hours in school, but that doesn't mean they're listening to the teacher.) How about the literacy level of the stuff they're absorbing through boob-tube, walkman, stereo-system, and non-academic printed word?

One difficulty in effecting any improvement in the use of English is the peculiar resistance to correction. We all make mistakes. I do, you do. No one is infallible. But for some reason, the faintest shadow of criticism of their grammar or pronunciation makes many people boil with rage. They will humbly consult experts on mar-riage problems, on child-rearing, dog-training, on repairing the car; but the mere suggestion that they're mispronouncing a word rouses them to fury. I'd rather be corrected than go on evoking derisive smiles behind the hand at my errors, but this is not usual practice.

When I was teaching English, correcting errors was my job, and I did it. Once in a while, on a sort of reflex, I corrected someone other than students. I never did this in public, but even in private it seemed to generate white-hot rage. I once suggested mildly to a friend that he was confusing "credulous" and "credible": he never forgave me. He resented it forever, though why it should occasion such wrath I still haven't figured out. He freely criticized my driving, my child-rearing methods, my French accent and my choice in clothes, and I sometimes found the criticism useful. (I sometimes found it irritating, but not impossible to transcend.) The suggestion that one's English might be faulty appears to be unforgivable.

Nevertheless, people who care about the language must not give up. We must fight on. Say not the struggle naught availeth. I propose to investigate the root cause of the complaint, and – who knows? – if we can make a diagnosis, isolate the cause of the affliction, we may yet discover a cure.

"The fight against bad English is not frivolous and is not the exclusive concern of professional writers." George Orwell, *Politics and the English Language*.

"There is one evil which . . . should never be passed over in silence but be continually publicly attacked, and that is corruption of the language . . . " W. H. Auden.

"Short words are best and the old words when short are best of all." Winston Churchill.

"Dat's a good woid!" private conversation.

1

Talking Classy

I first became aware that something dangerous was happening in English usage when, as a graduate student, I worked part-time marking undergraduate essays for one of my professors.

In the course of my labours, I turned up a great deal of support for Orwell's statement that English is in a bad way. A few prime examples:

1. "Johnson, Herbert, Maxwell, and Herrick all seem to place love on an elevated ptloemical level." [Maxwell turned out to be the author of the well-known poem, "To His Coy Mistress."]

2. "In the Pardoner's Tale, we are shown that Chaucer, like most people of his time, had an incomplete knowledge of animals, as he refers to snakes stinging instead of biting, and mentions the basilicae, an imaginary serpent of awesome powers."

3. ". . . Tennyson, who wrote to the memory of his beloved brother-in-law, Arthur Henery Hallman, his most famous poem, *In Memoran-dum.*"

4. "The Romantic period feauturing Keats, Shelley, Scott and Woods-worth, is, in my opinion, strangely void of animal lore.

5. "In 'Antony and Cleopatra' Shakesphere shows us a real physical love. Cleopatra is to coin a phrase a siren in every effect . . . A vasillating character with intrinsickally sexuous interests but with many facets to a truly very intriguing character, she represents the epitimy of human physical love and beauty. This is enormous heroic organic love. Love torn by conflict. Cleopatra shows us love, lust,

luxery, and corruptibility; she is a Goddess. Yet she is human is she not? Devious, petty, dignity, ruthless, canivoring, are a few of her more pronounced qualities. Hence is Cleopatra a true Loveable Lady."

Three different contributors announced that Cleopatra was an absolute oxymoron. Whether this resulted from collaboration or some serendipitous accident, I was unable to determine.

I had previously been confined (until I established my competence) to the laborious efforts of embryo pharmacists and agriculture students who did not try to conceal their total boredom with English courses, or their conviction that studying poets like "Woodsworth" and "Coalridge" was a waste of time that could be more profitably spent in the laboratory or stables. They were blunt, honest, and stodgy. Their spelling was shocking, their style generally uninspired, but they usually managed to make some sort of sense, and they did it briefly and unpretentiously. They accepted correction with weary patience.

As a reward for my labours with them, I was allowed to start marking Honours English candidates. It was from their effusions that the above quotations were gleaned. The same people who perpetrated these horrible examples were the very ones who were most glib with pretentious terminology like metonymy, aposiopesis, zeugma. Most of them, I was distressed to learn, were planning to go into teaching. That kind of thing – aposiopesis *et al.* – puts many kids off English for life.

Why were they writing this awful stuff? After a long period of bafflement, I was able to identify the cause, upon discovery of the following: "I will first explain how I prepose to utalize some simplistic parameters on which I have based this criteria on."

I called the perpetrator of this in to discuss his essay. He was proud, not apologetic.

"It sounds a lot classier if you use big words," he explained.

I had isolated and identified the Classy syndrome.

"It isn't classy," I argued, "if you mispronounce words and don't know what they mean or how to spell them."

Wasting my breath. He was wedded to polysyllables, regardless of their meaning. He believed that ordinary words, simple language, were signs of inferiority and naïveté. "Talking Classy" is a linguistic disease, spreading its malignancy everywhere – in newscasts, editorials, reportage, political speeches, classrooms – infecting both the written and the spoken word.

I gave a failing mark to the original Classy Specialist, but my boss raised his mark arbitrarily, saying that I marked too hard. My criticisms were making relations with his students difficult. That is, popularity was more important than the literacy of his graduates.

I had nightmares at the thought of the Apostle of Classy becoming an English teacher, and spreading his gospel of verbiage far and wide. Could he be responsible for the present ubiquity of the infection? No doubt he did his bit, but it's too big to be blamed on any one individual. It's a general trend. Talking classy is the linguistic equivalent of bad currency. According to Gresham's Law, ". . . the worst form of currency in circulation regulates the value of the whole currency and drives all other forms of currency out of circulation." The same principle applies in language, where the bad invariably drives out good.

These Classyists were first year students; they might learn, by graduation-time, to spell Shakespeare and know the difference between Woodsworth and Wordsworth, but would they ever get over the ghastly pretentiousness, the pseudo-scholarly jargon? How could they teach when they couldn't spell, couldn't write a coherent sentence? And oh God, their condescension! One of them accused Chaucer of logorrhoea. How I yearned for my Aggies, and the fine critical mind who said simply that the Pardoner made him want to puke.

The logorrhoea lady simply may have wanted to show off that big flashy word – but what did she gain? Chaucer is not guilty of it. He has a quite striking gift for economy that many contemporary writers might profitably imitate. "Thus swyvèd was the carpentere's wife," he says briskly, of an incident over which modern writers would expend dozens of sweaty pages. What the essayist really meant, of course, was that she was finding Chaucer difficult; instead of admitting this was her problem, and knuckling down to do the necessary work, she tried to shift the blame to Chaucer. An old ploy, familiar to teachers, but she made herself ridiculous by the use of that big pretentious word. Logorrhoea, just for the record, is a kind of verbal diarrhoea; it usually occurs in certain forms of mental illness – that *rhoea* suffix means "excessive flow". It is not appropriately used in literary criticism.

Sometimes in feverish nightmares I find myself suspecting that it is a conspiracy, a plot by some fiendish *éminence grise*, some linguistic Dr. Moriarty who, for God knows what evil motives, seeks to destroy the language. He has for years been sending out a secret vanguard, carefully trained to corrupt and destroy.

How else, for example, would you account for the take-over of "eck cetera"? No one said that when I was a student. Everyone was able to perceive that *et* must be pronounced ET, to rhyme with *get* (except in French, of course, where it rhymes – roughly – with *hey*). Nowadays most of North America insists on eck cetera, and I know where at least some of it started.

I once taught in a high school where the head of the English department managed to work an eck cetera into almost every sentence. (He was also jubilant about nucular esculation.)

How did he get to be head of a big English department? Why had he not been caught in university by some professor, and penalized brutally while he was still an impressionable student?

This head of a large English department did not have a degree in English. He was a Phys. Ed. major. He knew so little about English literature that he was an occupational hazard, a public nuisance. But he was a golfing buddy of the school principal, a math specialist who had always hated English, and figured that you didn't really have to know anything to teach it.

Other members of the department used to spend hours plotting to reform Our Leader's pronunciation. It was like the mice conferring on means of belling the cat: obviously it needed to be done, but who was actually to perform the deed? The faintest breath of criticism made him seethe with rage; he was – rightly – perennially suspicious of mutiny. He was the Captain Queeg of pedagogy. (Dat's a good woid. I'll explain "good woids" in a minute.)

We had chronic problems with the curriculum, under his guidance, because he furiously resisted the introduction of material with which he was unfamiliar; since he never read anything, this severely limited course content. (He had begun teaching English after he got too old for the playing fields. It was in the days of the provincial Grade 13 examination, and his method of teaching English was to go over old exam papers all year; that is, he taught exam-writing, not English. When they dropped the provincial examination, he was lost.)

It was pointed out that our students would be handicapped if they arrived in university with no knowledge of T. S. Eliot or W. B. Yeats or James Joyce. Our Leader grew restive at such suggestions. He was particularly resistant to Eliot, condemning Prufrock eck cetera as incomprehensible.

"I don't understand it," he was wont to say, "and if *I* don't understand it, why should we expect the students to understand it? And I," he invariably added, while we all held our breath in anticipation, "am the Head of this Department!"

The most recent author he had read was Somerset Maugham, who (he claimed) had brought the English novel to its greatest flowering. He had nothing but contempt for Joyce – not that he'd read Joyce, of course. Our Hero didn't need to read books to know they were no good.

He may not have invented eck cetera, but he certainly handed it on to generations of kids, some of whom became English teachers.

As long as English teachers are chosen for their golf game instead of their academic qualifications, and as long as school boards appoint principals who follow such practices, English will continue in jeopardy. Education will continue in jeopardy.

In another school where I taught, or tried to, it was believed that *anyone* could teach English: We all talk it, don't we? Here's a book, get in there and teach it.

The place was stuffing with sad young men who yearned to be out on the football field, but who had been thrust unceremoniously into a class-room, armed only with a book on *How To Teach English*. They were miserable, the kids were miserable, and no one learned anything. I was once required to "inspect" one of these teachers; discussing his problems with him after the class, or fiasco, I discovered that he didn't know what a participle was.

No one dies because they are unfamiliar with participles, but it's a bad sign in an English teacher. He was a whizz at football. I was pretty good at English. No one, however, would have dreamed of sending me out to coach the football team. It's not like English: you have to know what you're talking about to coach football.

While we're on the subject, let's clear up poor old et cetera, or etc. It means, literally, "and other things". *Et* is Latin for *and*. If you say "and cetera" you're mixing up English and Latin to the detriment of both; if you say "and et cetera", you are saying "and and other things". You can avoid the whole mess by simply saying "and so forth", or "and the rest of it/them". Alas, these nice easy English phrases aren't classy enough for Classy Speakers.

Very well. My first nominee for the degradation of English is the Talking Classy syndrome.

Other categories, to be dealt with later, include the decline in the teaching of grammar. Next, perhaps, redundancy; this may be a variation of Talking Classy. If extra syllables have more class, then unnecessary words may also be considered an ornament. Inappropriate euphemisms, hackneyed expressions, jargon, mixed metaphors, all the uglies noted by Orwell are still with us. Yet another pain-producer is Foreign Classy (aka the Per Se Complex), in which discourse is ornamented with foreign phrases, usually mispronounced, misspelled, and misused.

All professions inevitably develop their own jargon, but the Classy syndrome, the ignorance of grammar, the addiction to redundancy manifest themselves in even the most exalted. They cut across all educational and social strata. It's an epidemic.

Finally, a category which Orwell never anticipated: indecent language. He several times mentioned "unprintable words", which he clearly intended literally, in the sense that they simply were not fit to appear in print. Alas, nowadays there are no unprintable words; the one-time impermissibles have taken over the language. I'm saving this for much later, to avoid it as long as possible: no fair skipping to get to the Naughty Bits.

Finally, to forestall an inescapable argument: I don't want to freeze the language into a rigid form. I don't want it carved in stone to satisfy the pedants. I know language must change and evolve. I just don't see any reason that it should always change for the worse.

For example: recently I heard a biologist use the verb *to locomote* – "These monkeys never learned to locomote." It sounded barbarous. However, I looked it up and discovered that scientists had needed a word to express various kinds of movement – walk, jump, climb, fly, whatever – and someone had coined "locomote." It was at first classified as slang, but was so useful that it is now an accepted form in scientific papers. This is different from "verbing-out", discussed later.

2

Dat's a Good Woid

A journalist colleague of mine could be relied on, whenever anyone trotted out something really Classy, like a virtuoso convolution or a case of logorrhoea, to respond, "Dat's a good woid!" It was always spoken in tones of warmest admiration; and yet it had an oddly deflating effect. I find myself echoing it frequently these days, while watching TV or listening to radio, as commentators discourse on viable parameters or make fulsome comments while walking down chimerical streets: "Hey, dat's a *good* woid!"

I've been told that my approach to Classy Talk will discourage people who are interested in new words, who want to expand their vocabularies, who enjoy experimenting with language; I don't want to discourage that, but Classy is not the way to go. Talking/Writing Classy is using words sloppily and inappropriately, without taking the trouble to find out what they mean or how they're pronounced.

3

Some Too Frequently Utilized Good Woids: A Collection of the Commonest Offences

"Why do you utilize 'utilize' when you could use 'use'?" I frequently wrote on essay papers.

If this tiresome habit were confined to students, there would be some hope of their outgrowing it. Unfortunately, utilize has become close to universal. Just listen to any radio or TV interview, or to any phone-in programme, and notice how many people utilize utilize, while trying to be simplistic, based on a viable criteria for this media. (One moment, while I wash out my word-processor with soap.)

Utilize is full of traps for the incompetent speller (utalize, utelize, utulize) whereas it is really quite difficult to misspell "use". I did have one student who made it "uise", but that boy was gifted – he misspelled *everything*. He didn't so much make mistakes in spelling as create a new language.

A few years ago, utilize was a joke-word, a class indicator like "dentures" or "serviette" in Nancy Mitford's England. It occurred when a Non-U speaker was trying to sound superior. (U = Upper Class.)

"Haven't you any fryers or broilers?" demanded a character in Peter de Vries' *Reuben, Reuben*.

"Had some," replied the non-U chicken farmer, employing Classy language to impress the customer, "but they bin all utilized up."

By utilizing utilize, you gain a couple of syllables, and if you think that makes you sound Classy, God bless you. You gain nothing in clarity or significance; in fact, you probably meant *use* in the first place. There is a very delicate nuance of difference in the meaning .

. . shall I tell? No, dammit, I won't; go and look it up yourselves. However, I'll vouchsafe this much: you're always safe with use, but not with utilize.

Furthermore, although everyone tries hard to be as simplistic as possible, the effort is misguided. (They scorn simple old "simple" as not Classy enough, but that's what they really mean.) Once they start being simplistic, however, everything gets complicated. Simplistic can mean "having to do with herbs and simples", which is not always easy to work into the conversation, or else it means, says the *Shorter Oxford*, "over-simplified: from *simplism* – affected simplicity; unjustifiable simplification of problem"; now why do you want to give an answer like that, you simp?

I know it's futile, that better people than I have fought in the cause and failed, but I must nevertheless raise my voice against the near-universal abuse of unique. Dauntless the slug-horn to my lips I set: YOU CAN'T SAY A THING IS KINDA UNIQUE. It is an indecency. What does unique mean, you insensitive clods? If a thing is unique, there is only one of it, like the phoenix. It cannot be "really very unique" because absolutes do not admit of modifiers, qualifiers or intensives. What you probably mean is that it's rather unusual. What's so wrong with saying something is unusual? Why degrade *unique* to meaninglessness? What will you do when you need to describe something as one of a kind, admitting no qualifiers? If you see a phoenix?

Just turned up a new one (overheard in a corridor): "Isn't that the uniquest thing you ever seen?"

Recently I heard a politician demand that the Prime Minister be required to give "a more fulsome answer" to some parliamentary question – a terrifying suggestion. Mr. Mulroney is fulsome enough as it is, in all conscience. Surely the man didn't really want an answer that was *more* "offensive to normal sensibilities; cloying by excess of flattery, servility, exaggerated affection," did he?

"Did he expect this fulsome a vindication?" inquired an interviewer on "The Journal", apropos of the report on the Donald Marshall case. Surely our top journalists don't need to Talk Classy.

Donald Marshall got a FULL vindication in the report, which was straightforward and hard-hitting, but in no sense cloying, excessive, disgusting by excess of flattery, or servility. For heaven's sake, what's wrong with saying "full"?

There was a day when newspapers demanded a high standard of

English from reporters and editors. A radio station where I once worked employed a lady who subjected every page of copy to a merciless scrutiny, and made you re-write it if you failed to come up to her uncompromising standards.

"Never use the word 'integral'," she once commanded me. "It is impossible for announcers to pronounce correctly. It always comes out as 'intregal'."

Talking Classy may have originated with people like my student, but it has become a media disease.

A few years ago, Peter Gzowski had a weekly feature in which he invited us to walk with him down "a chimerical street". From the context, I assumed he meant a fantasy street – but that wasn't what he said. A chimerical street is no place to invite a lot of people who never did you any harm. It would be a walk down Nightmare Alley, for while a chimera may be a fantasy, it is never an agreeable one. It is, or was, a fire-breathing monster with a goat's head, a lion's body, and a serpent's tail; it was killed by Bellerophon, and a good thing, too. It can also be a mere wild fancy, an unfounded conception. Whichever it is, I don't want to walk down any street where chimeras might be encountered. Milton equipped hell with a batch of them – "gorgons and hydras and chimeras dire."

A hostess on CBC's "Four to Six" show inquired of a theatrical producer about the problems of introducing "a porcine" into his cast. She meant a pig. Why not say pig? There is no such thing as a porcine, because porcine is an adjective. It means piggish. No one would ask about introducing "a piggish", but the lady thought porcine sounded kind of uptown, I'll bet. The intention was mildly facetious, no doubt, but it nevertheless illustrates the insidious effect of the Classy syndrome: ignore simple (but correct) pig, and substitute Classy (but incorrect) porcine . . . and make it ridiculous.

Among the linguistic chimeras that I've noted lately are a few phrases that are invariably used incorrectly: *Begging the question* and *on behalf of.* Begging the question is currently being used, or rather misused, when the speaker means prompting the question, or leading to the question; they think it means that the question is begging to be asked. "If Mario Lemieux can't play centre because of his back, it begs the question whether he'll be willing to go to defence." Sports writers and broadcasters (with a few honourable exceptions) are great question-beggars, great exponents of Classy in general. They do not, unfortunately, believe in dictionaries, and they have an unerring capacity for picking up and incorporating in their vocabularies every misuse and abuse of language that comes into currency.

"Begging the question" is a term from logic. It means "to assume a proposition which, in reality, involves the conclusion." The classic illustration of a begged question is "Have you stopped beating your wife?", which assumes that you are in fact a wife-beater; if you answer no, it means that you are still beating your wife. If you answer yes, you're admitting that you have beaten her in the past.

On behalf of – misused with many exotic variations, such as "without his behalf". If you act on behalf of someone, you act in their interest, for their benefit. A counsellor will appear at a court hearing on behalf of a battered wife. In Classy circles, it seems to be taking on the totally inappropriate meaning of "on the part of", with a suggestion of diabolical machination. "It was because of Peter Pocklington's behalf that the Oilers lost Wayne." And, "There was a real uproar on behalf of the audience when the band didn't show up till ten o'clock." Who created the uproar, if not the audience? Who else was there, to act on behalf of the audience, for its benefit or in its interest? Why not say "by the audience" or "on the part of the audience"? Because, I'm afraid, there is some dim idea floating about that "behalf" has more class.

Sometimes these misuses make it almost impossible to determine what the speaker is trying to say. "This latest move on the behalf of Iraq is going to complicate the plans for a ground war," announced a television reporter. (February 15, 1991.) But nobody seemed to be acting on behalf of Iraq – they were all lined up on the other side, eager to bomb the Iraqis into oblivion. Iraq had just made a tentative peace offer: did the journalist mean the latest move by Iraq, or on the part of Iraq? Then why in tunket couldn't she say so, instead of saying the opposite? Why doesn't she check it in a dictionary, or Fowler's *English Usage?*

"There was a smattering of familiar faces in the crowd," advised a "colour" reporter at a recent event, and later she told about a "smattering" of applause. I'm not sure what word she was reaching for – spatter? scattering? Something fairly sparse, from the context. But that isn't what smattering means. It's a "slight, superficial knowledge of language or subject". To smatter is to talk ignorantly, or prate.

11

No word is Classier today than eclectic, which is generally mis-used to mean something like heterogeneous. "An eclectic crowd turned out for the meeting, with representatives from every ethnic group in the city." But eclectic really means something like selective – one has eclectic taste in music if one enjoys both Mozart and Fats Waller. Instead of being limited and narrow in one's choice, one is eclectic, choosing without fear of academic censure to read Chaucer or Damon Runyon (who actually have a good deal in common). If you try to read, or listen to, or admire, only that which is officially approved as Okay Music/Literature/whatever, you are non-eclectic, and missing a lot of fun.

These are only a few of the most commonly occurring instances of Classy speech and writing, only a few of hundreds. I've probably missed some of the worst, and failed to hit on the *bêtes noires* of many literate sufferers. But at least it gives the general idea of the plague afflicting our language.

"Cultivate simplicity," Charles Lamb once wrote to Coleridge; it must have taken a lot of nerve, and I wish I knew what Coleridge replied. He may have told the gentle essayist something unprint-able, in Orwellian terms. Nevertheless, it was sound advice then, and it's sound still.

4

Oh, Say, CBC . . .

The Canadian Broadcasting Corporation was once a model for all of us, but its writers and many of its reporters and announcers seem to have lost their dictionaries. Some of them may never have heard of dictionaries. I'm still an incurable CBC listener, for which reason it may seem perverse of me to be picking on the old Air Mother: she's the source of a great many of my Horrible Examples. No doubt if I listened to the commercial stations I would reap an even more abundant harvest, but I would almost certainly have perished in the course of the work.

I remain faithful to the CBC, partly because I'm spared commercials, and partly from habit. It is no longer a reliable model for good English, I'm afraid, but some of the deterioration may be attributable to the Mulroney government's policy of progressively starving it into non-functioning. (Not being able to afford a dictionary, among other deprivations.) When it's past saving, the P.M. will sell it to "direct public ownership", Michael Wilson's term for exploitation by private interests, where our broadcasting system will join our railway system, Petro-Can, Air Canada, the Film Board, and (soon) the Post Office.

I've also been accused of unfairness to the Toronto *Star* and the Hamilton *Spectator.* There are probably lots of worse newspapers, but I usually read the *Star* and the *Spec*, which is my local daily. The same bad habits – and possibly worse – can effortlessly be found in publications everywhere.

Nevertheless, if you join the Fourth Estate, in however humble or exalted a capacity, you have an obligation to use good English. If you set a bad example, the effects are incalculable. You're every bit as responsible for the quality of the English spoken in this country as anyone in the educational field. You should know, for example, the difference between *acronym* and *anachronism,* as a certain prominent radio personality doesn't: an acronym is a word made up of initial letters of other words. LASER is an acronym for Light Amplification of Stimulated Emission of Radiation. (It's also a gum resin mentioned by Roman writers, made from an umbelliferous plant; bet you didn't know *that!* Neither did I, until this morning.) An *anachronism,* however, is an error in computing time; attribution of an event, custom, or circumstance to a wrong period of time. The most famous one is that clock striking, in *Julius Caesar,* before clocks had been invented.

Another announcer, and one of the best, made a strange gaffe on a "Sunday Morning" broadcast. She referred to "the Shakespearean song, 'Now is the winter of our discontent . . .'" That's not a song, that's the opening line of Richard III, from the villain's marvellous soliloquy, in which he announces his shameless plans to seize the crown.

Why don't I identify the perpetrators of these errors, as I have exposed others? Because most of the time they're excellent, providing reliable models of sound English usage. Everyone has a right to one or two errors, without being jumped on. It's the shameless repeat-offender who deserves to be named and nailed. Another reason for not identifying perpetrators is my incompetent methodology. When I hear an atrocious abuse of language, I write it down, usually on the table-cloth, after which I tend to go into shock and fail to note name, time, date, etc., so that I can't properly document the atrocity. I give you my word, however, that I'm not making them up. I *couldn't* make them up, and if it were necessary to make them up, I wouldn't have to go to all the work of writing this book.

"I agree with you," wrote George Rich, the manager of the Broadcast Language Department of the CBC, in response to my complaints, "that it is customary for many of us to place the blame on the education system when we hear poor English usage. It is my belief that every broadcaster is in reality a teacher, and I've been trying to make broadcasters aware of the responsibility they have in regard to the correct use of language."

You have to try harder, George! Some of those teachers are doing a shockingly bad job.

I repeat: if you're going to work in the media, and set up as an authority, don't think you'll get away with being slovenly. Don't, because you have a degree in journalism, assume that you can rest on your laurels, and that your English is good enough. *We're listening, and watching you!*

5

English Grammar: As It Lays Dyeing

Over the years, in all of the media as well as in private conversation, there has been a steady erosion of good English.

In extenuation, it must be admitted that English is not a consistent language. It is full of traps for the unwary, such as copula verbs which govern the nominative where you'd normally expect the accusative. That is, when someone calls from the living-room, "Who's that in the kitchen?", you're supposed to answer, instead of the normal "Smee," the unnatural "It is I." I suspect this rule was made up by some old pedant in the 19th century, like the rules for the uses of shall and will. It's one of the cases where I simply ignore the rules and go with what Fowler's *English Usage* calls "comfortable."

Besides, the verb "to be" is irregular to the point of schizophrenia, booby-trapped with perils for the stumbling grammarian. "An irregular and defective verb," says the *Shorter Oxford* severely, "the full conjugation of which is made up of the surviving inflexions of three verbs . . ."

In spite of occasional anomalies of this sort, we all need to understand how our language works, and the only way to do it is to learn its grammar. Not for snobbish reasons, to sound "U" (for Upper Class), but in order to communicate effectively.

I don't believe in grammatical rules unless they have some point or reason. The essentials of effective communication are clarity, precision, and if possible, some degree of style and grace.

No one wants ordinary spoken English to be formal and rigidly correct: God forbid. Nor does anyone want solemn pedantic language in the media, especially in unrehearsed impromptu speech. We do want to hear *good* English, even though it is casual and conversational. It can be slangy and colloquial, but NOT illiterate or pretentious.

Good language habits, once formed, usually persist in all circumstances. Even though the situation is informal and unrehearsed, literate people aren't going to start saying "I seen" and "I've went"; they've learned their irregular verbs, and they don't reserve them exclusively for public occasions. They speak grammatically both in private and public.

A stricter set of standards is required for written language, except in dialogue. An occasional error on live productions is inevitable, although an interviewer who habitually uses good English is far less likely to make hideous gaffes than someone who never uses a dictionary, or has never learned any grammar. Newscasts on radio and TV are written in advance, and presumably edited, and so should avoid outrageous errors. Nevertheless, the most blench-making solecisms occur in the news, in spite of which announcers read them without a blench: "Five people was injured in traffic accidents during the storm . . ." "One criteria for excellence is performance . . ."

I remember grinding my teeth when several newscasts repeated the solemn fact that, prior to the funeral of our former Governor General, Jules Léger, he was for several days *laying in state* . . . Could no one have picked up on this inexcusable gaffe and eliminated it after the first exposure? Apparently not.

Where do they find these allegedly professional writers, who haven't assimilated the most basic elements of English grammar and usage? A good many of them are university graduates, but a degree is no longer any guarantee of a high level of literacy.

If we try to identify the culprit, we find ourselves in an endless process of buck-passing. The universities blame the high schools and the high schools blame the public schools. We all blame bad parents and peer pressure. I blame the media, as well as the education system. Watching television instead of reading books has clearly contributed significantly to incompetence in reading.

Grammar was once taught rigorously in public and high schools. It was difficult to teach, and many kids hated it. It required endless drill and exercises. Nevertheless, it trained people to understand the structure of language, and it is this which we are missing now.

Unhappily, some time in the permissive climate of the Sixties, influenced by a misinterpretation of Marshall McLuhan, a good many schools decided it wasn't necessary to teach grammar. They also adopted ill-advised methods for teaching reading, and almost precluded the mastery of spelling.

Soon we were graduating teachers who couldn't spell, and whose grammar was rudimentary: the contagion spread like the Black Death, contaminating generation after generation. Children brought home report-cards full of errors in grammar and spelling *by the teacher.* "Geoff is full of curiousity," observed one of his mentors. Another described my niece as being "exceptionally unique" in her ability to write stories.

When I began to prepare myself to be a school-marm, I got some severe shocks. One of my instructors in the Ontario College of Education solemnly warned us against teaching the difference between the verbs "to lie" and "to lay". The reason was that the filthy-minded little beasts of students would be so convulsed with hilarity, because of the colloquial applications of the verb to lay, that it would be impossible to keep order.

"You'll have a riot on your hands," he cautioned us, "if you start talking about 'lay' in the – uh – transitive sense." Some of us refused this defeatist counsel. My method was to short circuit the hilarity by recounting my instructor's warning about the salacious-mindedness of students. They scoffed at the idea that they (so cool, so worldly-wise) could possibly be amused by anything so primitive.

"The verb to lay," murmured a languid Grade 13 sophisticate, "oh, hardee-har-har."

Most of my colleagues, unfortunately, observed the warning. The verb *to lie* (v. intr., to be in a recumbent or prostrate position) has disappeared from the vocabulary of all save a dwindling minority. And of course the rot didn't begin with that generation. In Judy La marsh's first novel, *A Very Political Lady*, the heroine – on the second page – is laying in bed.

Judy was a lawyer, an M.P., a cabinet member. She should have known better. And surely some editor should have jumped on it before it got into print?

"What did you lay, an egg?" That was the riposte with which my old Grade Five teacher crushed everyone who committed that particular crime. But in these degenerate days, our Governor General can lay in state through three newscasts, uncorrected, and no voice is raised in rebuke or protest.

The participle "laying" has become a kind of test case, a literacy indicator: anyone who admits to laying around or laying in bed all day is inadequately literate even if he/she has a Ph.D. – and some of the guilty parties do.

Indulge me: let me set out for one last time, before I'm too old and frail, the reasons for the tragic lie/lay confusion. Three verbs should be mentioned. First is the verb to lie in the sense of telling a falsehood. It is one of the few regular verbs in English, giving no trouble to anyone.

The root, or infinitive, is to lie; present participle, lying; past tense, lied; past participle, lied. I lie today, I lied yester day; I was lying for years before that; I have lied, in fact, ever since I learned to talk, liar that I am.

Next verb is *to lay*, meaning to place or deposit, to put something down, and a variety of seldom used applications. Its most common application is in the case of a bird, or possibly a reptile, laying an egg; a royal person laying a foundation stone; or, in the colloquial (allegedly hilarious) sense, of having sexual intercourse with someone. Ghosts are also laid, without sexual implications.

This verb is very nearly regular: To lay; laying; laid; laid. The speaker in the following example is a hen. "I lay eggs. I was laying eggs yesterday, I'm laying an egg right now, I'll be laying or will lay eggs tomorrow. I laid an egg yesterday. I have laid eggs every day since I was a mere pullet."

The verb *to lay* is transitive; that is, it takes an object. You can't just lay there, you have to lay something. You can't be laying, unless you are laying something, or someone (har). However, it can be used reflexively: Now I lay me down to sleep.

The Gresham syndrome is of course at work here, making bad grammar universal; the Perversity Principle is also at work. I heard the ultimate instance on CBC's "Prime Time", October 4, 1990: "I lie myself down." He could have used "lay" there, and been correct; but no, sir, the instinct to pick the wrong word is unerring. The misuse of "lay" is chronic and near-universal, but when it happens to be correct they throw it out and misuse "lie."

The confusion arises with the verb *to lie*, meaning to recline, to be in a prostrate or recumbent position. This verb is irregular, with frightful consequences. It is also intransitive, meaning that it doesn't take an object. It's the source of all our troubles, because its past tense is *lay*– with no object. Remember that, if you lay in bed all day yesterday, you don't have to worry about the verb taking an object. Remember, also, that it is against the law, punishable by hideous tortures, to say that you laid in bed all day yesterday: that takes us back to those infernal eggs.

Principal parts of this monster are as follows: Infinitive, to lie; present participle, lying (not laying!); past tense, lay (not laid!); past participle, lain (not laid!). Correctly used thus: I like to lie in bed; I lie in bed every night. I like lying in bed, especially when I should have been up hours ago, earning an honest living. Yesterday I lay in bed all morning; I was lying there until noon. Sometimes I have lain in bed for days on end.

No approval of such idle habits is implied, but grammatically the usage is correct.

At the risk of being repetitive, I will repeat: this verb is intransitive. It does not take an object. The present participle is lying, *lying*, LYING, *LYING*– not laying. Bob Dylan's loathesome song should go "Lie, lady, lie –" unless of course the lady is laying that damned egg. And if she is, why doesn't he say something about it? The past tense is LAY, *not laid*, and in the past tense it doesn't need an object. The past participle is LAIN, *not laid*.

Whenever you find yourself using the words *laying* or *laid*, hastily ask yourself, *Laying what? Laid what?* Suppose you have laid something undesirable, like a basilisk's egg? (In Classy, a basilicae's egg.) Think of the embarrassment.

I know I'm wasting my time, and that all of this will make no difference, but I must make one last pitiful effort before I go hence and am heard no more.

There are many other irregular verbs which lead to deplorable locutions: I've went, I seen, I done. These used to be unerring indicators of educational deprivation. Now we hear them everywhere. ("You done good, kid," is permissible with facetious intent; should perhaps be followed by "har har" or noises to that effect, to indicate that one knows better.)

Shall we pause on this trio for a moment? (I won't do the lie/lay thing.) These three verbs are also dead give-aways of a weak grammatical background. Their difficulty arises from an irregularly formed past tense.

Thus we have, go – went – gone; see – saw – seen; do – did – done. So when you're talking about something in the past, you don't say "he done" or "I seen". If you're using the past participle, you have to help it along with an auxiliary, *have* or *had*. I have gone, I have seen, I have done. If it's a simple past, however, you say, I went, I saw, I did. NEVER I've went, I've saw, I've did.

What do I mean, regular and irregular verbs? A regular verb forms its past tense and past participle simply by adding *d* or *ed*. But most verbs are irregular, and they follow no reliable pattern. A regular verb is destroy – destroyed – destroyed.

Even with something as easy as that, the perversity principle gets to work. The compulsion to mess it up is apparently irresistible.

"We can't let one team destruct the whole league." That's CBC sports again. The verb is destroy. The derived noun is destruction, but there's no excuse for working back from destruction to invent a monstrosity like destruct.

"At this time of year [Easter] we think of Jesus trodding the road to Calvary." You won't catch me thinking that. There is no verb *to trod*. It's tread, you semi-literate cleric. Tread, treading, trod, trodden. How can someone get through a course in theology and come out saying "trodding"? How can you write a "Report on Business" for the Toronto *Star*? Edward Greenspan (November 22, 1989 p. B4), describes the path "that the Soviet Union now is trodding".

A recently discovered horror is "to smote", instead of to smite – CBC again. Smite, smiting, smote, smitten. Smote is the past tense, not the infinitive. These abuses cause me real, actual, physical pain.

It's all unnecessary. In the generation preceding mine, university educations were the privilege of the rich. Neither of my parents went to university, in spite of which they both spoke and wrote excellent English. Neither of them made errors in spelling or grammar, which they learned in public school. They may have been above average because they were both great readers (though not avid ones), but in general, the level of English among people who were not downright deprived was better then than it is now, when almost everyone has some post-secondary education.

To wit: "Anyways, like I said . . ."

The speaker was a colleague of mine, a teacher in the English department of a Community College. I thought dreamily back to a day, not terribly remote, when I had been working on a play for

CBC and had wanted to indicate that a character was (how to put it unsnobbishly?) non-U, of the people, educationally underprivileged. The device I adopted, with the approval of the director, was the line, "Anyways, like I said . . ."

Now here it was, on the lips of one who was charged with the instruction of the young. And not just any old instruction: instruction in *English*, goddammit, and no one was objecting.

"Hey, you," I said, raising my voice, "watch your language." He looked at me in mild surprise; even when I explained that he was doing abominable things to the language I loved, he was not at all offended. "Do you still bother with stuff like that?" he asked, rather interested, as an anthropologist might be in discovering the survival of some quaint archaic custom.

I still bother, though I often wonder if it's worth the trouble. When all the rest of the world is just laying there, letting the language go all to hell, why should I go on fighting? Everyone in the world will soon say laying for lying, I believe, except me.

What's wrong with *anyways?* You're making something plural when the intention is singular – any way you want to look at it. All the authorities I've consulted agree on this: no *s*. Maxwell Nurnberg's useful (and entertaining) *Questions You've Always Wanted To Ask About English But Were Afraid to Raise Your Hand* says, "Anyways, anywheres, somewheres, everywheres: There should be no *s* at the end of any of these words. *Avoid*: 'It's a long ways from here.'"

You can say "ways" if you genuinely intend the plural – to wit, "There are many ways by which you can improve your English."

What's wrong with "like I said"? Let me draw a long breath before I embark on this complicated matter, which should have been explained step-by-step long ago in public school. In all languages, there are structures called phrases and clauses. "I keep my money in the bank." *In the bank* is a phrase. Phrases are introduced by prepositions: *in* is a preposition. Phrases do not have verbs. If it has a verb, it's a clause.

"I keep my money in the bank, where it is safe." *Where it is safe* is a clause. Clauses are introduced by conjunctions: *where* is a conjunction. Clauses have verbs – in this case, *is*.

Like is a preposition. Correct use: "He looks like his father." If the construction contains a verb, it's a clause. "Like I said" contains a verb; it's a clause. You need a conjunction to introduce it, and so "like I said" won't do. You must say, *as* I said.

Efforts at correcting these regrettable habits often produce undesirable results. People are told that such constructions as "like I said" are classed as vulgarisms, and should be avoided. They don't grasp the grammatical principles, but decide that there is some virtue in conjunctions that prepositions lack (Classier) and start using conjunctions everywhere. Thus Christie Blatchford writes, "He generally behaved as a juvenile delinquent." (Toronto *Sun*, January 28/ 90). "As a juvenile delinquent" has no verb, and so is not a clause, and so should not be introduced by the conjunction *as*. He behaved LIKE a juvenile delinquent.

Anyways like I said is – along with the intransitive use of laying – the most conspicuous example of the contagious effect of bad grammar. A generation ago, these errors were unmistakeable indicators of educational deprivation. Now they are used by university graduates, who wonder why anyone bothers about that stuff.

"If I would have been able, I'd have gone to the concert." Why that "would have"? (Frequently, "would of", just to make things worse.) It's totally unnecessary. Just say, "If I had been able, I'd have gone to the concert." This is one of the most frequently recurring grammatical errors today, and it's quite new: I heard it first only two or three years ago. "If he would have quit drinking sooner, the accident wouldn't never have happened." It's spreading like cancer. Correct version: "If he had quit drinking sooner, the accident would never have happened." (Don't use double negatives.)

The explanation of this is complicated and I'm not going to write it out. If you really want to know why you shouldn't use that *would have* in the subordinate clause, get an old-fashioned grammar text and study it for yourself. The rule is generally that the action in the subordinate (if) clause happens *before* – or should have happened before – that in the main clause. You therefore want the past tense. Remember: never *would have* in both clauses.

Would of, should of, had of ... orally they're almost indistinguishable from *would have*, etc. Inexcusable on the printed page, however. Please note, William Thomas of the Hamilton *Spectator* – "... if he had of been pitching against Philadelphia ..."

Different than: "That's a bit different than the original version." My spine creeps at the sound. Would you say, "It differs than the original version"? I hope not. You can differ with someone: that is, you don't agree with them – or you can differ from them, i.e., simply be unlike them. Be different from them. I haven't the faintest hope that this will ever be reformed. Another cancer. It's epidemic on CBC.

Than what: "They can get better deals than what the government is offering them," said Alana Campbell on the six o'clock news (26 January, '90). Why is that "what" stuck in there? "We're selling more gas than what Canada can produce." Remove the *whats*: "better deals than the government is offering" – what's wrong with that? "more gas than Canada can produce". Perfectly good constructions. Why add that quite unnecessary and ugly "what"? Cancer three. Note: Michael Wilson, our infamous ex-finance minister, on top of all of his other crimes, is an inveterate "than what" user.

Equally as: It's equally silly to stick in an unnecessary *as*, as to add a superfluous *what*. "It's equally silly." That says it. You don't need that *as*. Start practising: *equally good, equally bad, equally big, equally small*, but for pity's sake, not *equally as*.

Perhaps we could organize a movement for the purification of language? For the survival of the participle "lying"? For the rescue of grammar? The elimination of *than what* and *different than*?

Does anyone care about the language – anyone, that is, except me and a few other elderly purists? There's no time to waste. When my contemporaries and I are gone, there'll be no one left who knows the difference between good English and bad, as witness the terrible crimes perpetrated by university professors and high school teachers, and all you types in the media.

Briefly, a few words that are so perfectly impossible that I really dislike writing about them: *irregardless* – non-U, possibly Classy because of that superfluous *ir*, for *regardless*. I really thought this one was beyond the pale, but I heard it only a few weeks ago on "Morningside". The word is *regardless*: add that *ir* and it's a double negative. The *ir* and the *less* cancel each other out.

It's another lost cause, but I will fight to the death against using an apostrophe to indicate a plural: "Many Senior Citizen's are living on reduced income's." And a shopping plaza sign offered Ladie's Swim Suits, indicating serious mental confusion. You can have either a lady's swim suit, or ladies' swim suits – enough for lots of ladies. But ladie's don't exist.

Belief in this indefensible use of the apostrophe has sneaked in everywhere; recently I saw a poster on which all the correct plurals had been circled, as if to indicate errors, and apostrophes carefully inserted with magic marker.

The apostrophe doesn't indicate a plural. It either indicates possession (The dog's tail is wagging) or an omission (That's my dog!). In the first case, the apostrophe is the vestige of a long lost possessive pronoun: "The dog, his tail . . ." In the second, the apostrophe denotes the omission of *is* – "That is my dog!"

CBC-TV used regularly to broadcast its ignorance of the function of the apostrophe on something called "Yuk Yuk's". If you have more than one Yuk Yuk, you've got Yuk Yuks, and God pity you.

Rules for correct apostrophe use are complicated, but they can be checked in any good grammar text. I'm not going to get into that. However, let's (for let us) look at a few trouble-makers.

Personal pronouns don't use an apostrophe for the possessive: *his, hers, yours, ours, theirs, its, whose,* are possessives by definition. So please spare us her's, your's, our's, their's. If you write *it's,* you are saying (briefly) *it is. Who's* is not a possessive, but the abbreviation for *who is.*

If a noun, whether singular or plural, does not end in *s,* add *'s*: children's; women's; men's. Proper names introduce complications: please consult *Questions You Always Wanted to Ask* etc.

One particular category of proper-name-cum-apostrophe abuse bothers me seriously, since I keep coming across it in books by British publishers from whom one expects better things. This is in the case of names ending in *s*: when speaking of a house occupied by the Smithers family, they've begun to identify it as the Smithers's. Try pronouncing that: it has to be Smithersuz.

Questions You've Always . . . suggests that with long words, and/ or those with more than one *s,* one should use the apostrophe alone. Thus, "Sophocles' seven tragedies, Archimedes' principle, Socrates' philosophy" . . . all of these are easy to say. But just listen to the terrible sound you make when you say Sophocles's.

Now a few miscellaneous monstrosities in sentence structure, courtesy of the Hamilton *Spectator*: Columnist Gerry Ormond inquires,

Are you sick and tired of pollution and non-recyclable *[sic]* spark plugs and rotten water you take your life in your hands if you drink and soot and acid rain?

Oh, I am indeed. But I am even more tired of sentences like that. Even if columnist Ormond is insensitive enough to perpetrate such a horror, wouldn't you think someone on the editorial staff would catch it? Fat chance.

The following is from an editorial insert above a *Spectator* wire-service story:

> The United States has at last switched who it supports in Cambodia, a country the U.S. has treated worse than it has treated any other nation ever, argues international affairs columnist William Pfaff.

Surely any self-respecting journalist would wince at having his name associated with such atrocities?

"Newfoundlanders need the money much moreso than Ontario workers." That was from the editorial page of one of our major dailies. "The ranges [of examination results] here are very much concentrated moreso." That was a school teacher; did she mean more concentrated? God knows. This malpractice arose because of misunderstanding of a minor grammatical point, where one uses "so" to avoid repetition of a long phrase. "The deficit was a heavy burden under the Liberals; under the Conservatives it is more so." Perfunctorily taught and half-heard, this has produced the unloveable moreso.

Why does bad English drive out good? It's as infectious as mumps, or chicken pox, whereas good English (if it isn't acquired by osmosis, in early life, through good example) has to be laboriously studied.

CHAPTER

6

From Whence These Apotheoses and Epiphanies?

The words in this collection of horrors are less common than those in the previous chapter, but they are much Classier. Although some would-be Classyists find them a trifle intimidating, they are nevertheless spreading rapidly, illustrating the Gresham's Law effect in language, of bad driving out good.

The fancier the misused word, the sillier the effect. Talking Classy can make you look a prize idiot. This struck me forcibly on reading in a glossy magazine (in the dentist's office) that former evangelist Charles Templeton had experienced an apotheosis.

"You can come in now," said the nurse, and I put the magazine down without making a note of name, author or date. All I remember is that it was a Canadian glossy. The villain must escape unidentified, but not unrebuked.

Now I yield to no one in awed respect for Mr. Templeton, but I decline to believe that he is God, or even a god. *Apotheosis* means deification, or being ranked among the gods. The article was discussing Templeton's defection from evangelism; possibly the writer meant he had had some kind of reverse religious experience, an agnostic revelation? But that isn't what he said. He said Charles had become a god. If you're going to use a big fancy word like that, you should at least find out what it means.

Apotheosis is very vogue-ish these days; you can hear it floating in the air at parties: "Hey, that's a regular apotheosis!" By the Gresham principle (Bad In, Good Out, or BIGO), the misuse spreads inexorably. Classyists have also jumped on epiphany, and

27

incorporated it into their dreadful vocabularies: "I keep having these epiphanies about how to re-decorate the bathroom." In pre-Classy days, epiphany meant "a manifestation or appearance of some divine or superhuman being", according to the *Shorter Oxford*; it has recently been permitted in the sense of inspiration, or a Eureka-like revelation. You might have a good idea for re-decorating the bathroom, but to call it an epiphany is to degrade the word, and to produce a very strange bathroom.

Associated with these words (has someone been reading, for no good purpose, Roget's *Thesaurus*?) are some other terms with vaguely revelatory associations. Perhaps it's the approaching millennium? Apocalypse and apocrypha are being used as decorations in many an uptown conversation. "The noise was positively apocryphal!" exclaimed a marvellous lady, reporting on a concert.

The Apocrypha is the term for books of the Old Testament included in the Septuagint and Vulgate, but not in the Hebrew Bible and not in modern Bibles. They were excluded from the Sacred Canon at the time of the Reformation by the Protestants. What kind of noise do non-canonical holy books make? Hard to imagine. By derivation, something apocryphal is "of doubtful authenticity; spurious". But not noisy at all.

Loud noises are sometimes (acceptably) described as apocalyptic, perhaps the word for which the lady was fumbling. The original apocalypse was the revelation accorded to St. John the Divine concerning the end of the world and the second coming of Christ; by extension, it's used of grand or violent events bearing some resemblance to St. John's vision. Literal believers of the Bible are convinced that the end of the world is imminent, probably coinciding with the end of this century and millennium, and this may have brought the words into popular use. The war in the Middle East is cited as evidence for fulfilment of the prophecy. I'll save my criticism of this theory for another book; suffice it to say that an apocalypse is a rackety affair, with storms, loud voices speaking out of the heavens, and mountains falling down . . . I daresay it could be used, at a stretch, to describe a rock concert.

A great favourite among the underprivileged religious aspiring to be Classy is "prophecize". It has attained wide circulation with the rise of the television evangelists, few of whom are noted for their command of good English. I believe they attend Bible colleges, where the curriculum is rather limited. They are very strong on prophecizing. In the unlikely event that any Born Agains may pick up this book, I offer this little mnemonic: Prophesy is a verb, prophecy a noun. How can you remember this? *Is* is a verb, and it's spelled with an *s*, as in the verb *prophesy. Ice* is a noun, and it's spelled with a *c*, as is the noun *prophecy.* There is no such word as "prophecize." Now do you think you can get it right? Probably not.

While we're on the Good Book, let's consider another very popular Classyism, "from whence?"

"Take back your mink/To from whence it came," sang Adelaide in *Guys and Dolls,* and (in the dim past) we laughed indulgently at her comic non-U attempt to sound cultured. Classy talkers jumped on it at once, and worked "from whence" into the conversation whenever possible or rather, whenever impossible. *Whence* means *from where?, from what source or place?,* so if you say "from whence" you're saying "from from what source or place?" Actually, Adelaide had an intimidating precedent to justify her Classy terminology – no less than the Bible itself: "I will lift up mine eyes unto the hills, from whence cometh my help." I feel a little anxious about arguing with an authority like that, and I have to admit that the effect is good; the "from" was needed for scansion. Nevertheless, in current use, the intention is almost invariably Classy. For other examples of this practice, see the chapter on redundancy. *Askance* is becoming very big in Classy circles. "Certain offences haven't been looked on with that much askance by the police," said a newscaster. You can't look on anything with askance, because askance isn't a noun, it's an adverb. You can *look askance*, because that describes *how* you look, one of the functions of an adverb. No doubt someone heard the word used, guessed at its approximate meaning, thought it sounded Classy, and decided to decorate his story, a practice on which I look (correctly) askance.

Chauvinism was once a useful word, meaning "exaggerated and bellicose patriotism". It derived from the name of Nicholas Chauvin, who went cuckoo in his excessive admiration for Napoleon. "Aggressive . . . nationalism, which exalts national consciousness and spreads hatred of other peoples." Feminists appropriated it, bracketing it with "male" and "pig", to designate extreme misogyny, or hatred of women. We did already have misogynist, but it had a languid theoretical quality; male chauvinist pig is much more vigorously evocative. Unfortunately, following a Classy take-over, chauvinism has completely lost its original meaning, with its nationalist connotation, and is now almost exclusively used to mean a woman-hater or abuser, so that we've lost a useful word and now have two (chauvinist, misogynist) meaning the same thing. Bad economy.

I'm not sure whether the next group belongs to the Classy syndrome or whether they are simple errors, in which verbs are mistakenly derived from nouns. Among the commonest are *commentate* and *orientate*. Perhaps the extra syllable is irresistible to the Classy writer? But why orientate one's self to a situation, if one can save a syllable and orient one's self? Presumably they have formed themselves backward from the noun: thus we have *to reforestate*, from reforestation, and – horrors! –*conversate* from conversation.

Another criminal act, recently called to my attention by a grieving mother, is the counterfeit *conferencing*, for discussion between teacher and student. Why can't you confer with the student, Teach? Not Classy enough?

Related to this is the practice of "verbing out" complained of by the editor of the *Manchester Guardian*:

> . . . the pressing of decent defenceless nouns, which have gone about their business for centuries without giving the mildest offence or provocation, into service as verbs, sometimes in their original form but quite often after a process of horrible mutilation.

He illustrates it from the "Today" programme on the BBC: "Let us example that for you."

"We are exiting the old year," the chairman of the ICI informed his employees, and the chairman of Chrysalis Groups announced that "Record levels [were] achieved in 1989 after expensing a significant investment in new talent." Yet another businessman complained of having to "diarise" his appointments. Sometimes business lunches are delayed while the wine is being "room-temperatured".

One of the earliest examples of this is enthuse. "I'm not enthused about moving to Winnipeg." Moved backwards from the noun enthusiasm, which everyone should look up in a good dictionary: a most surprising word. I've hardly dared to use it since I looked it up, because it's so totally unlike what I'd assumed it to mean. I'm not going to tell you, though: you must look it up yourself.

The grisliest example of verbing-out was drawn to my attention by a friend, who has heard it three times lately on TV. It's *incested*, as in "The child was incested by her father."

Perhaps the easiest way of tackling the rest of my Classy collection is to arrange the items alphabetically.

Avid: It breaks the Classy rule by being a short word, but it is misused to mean keen, enthusiastic, dedicated. In fact, it simply means greedy or grasping – not a nice thing to say about anyone. I heard a friend of mine once described as "an avid child-worker". It is possible that the word for which avid-users are reaching is ardent. An ardent devotee of the theatre makes sense, an avid one is simply idiotic. I was once described in a biographical note as "an avid skier" – a greedy or grasping skier? I wouldn't mind being called an ardent skier, though in fact I'm not. I just like messing around on skiis on nice sunny winter days. But I digress. While the *Shorter Oxford* refuses to countenance any meaning except greedy or grasping, a few authorities make a concession for *eager*; the instances cited, however, seem always to be associated with the trough. Not eagerness to help others, or even to go skiing, but to pig out.

Cacophony: This is enjoying an enormous vogue among people who don't know what it means, how to pronounce it, or how to spell it. It was pronounced as if the second "o" were an "a" – cacaphony – by a well-known folk singer during a CBC interview in which she talked at length about her acute sensitivity to words. Another splendid Classy cacophony turned up in print: Jeanne McDowell, writing in *Time* (where they can't afford a dictionary), about Earth Day celebrations, advised that ". . . in thousands of communities around the world, citizens will stage a cacophony of events [such as] tree plantings, bicycle parades . . ." (December, '89). Funny kind of environmental celebration, producing world-wide noise pollution. She got the spelling right, but obviously didn't know what the word meant. Cacophony, Jeanne, and *Time* editors, means "a harsh or ill sound; discordant combination of sound; moral discord". Do you really think that's suitable for celebrating Earth Day? And wouldn't it be a good idea to find out what it means before writing your article? She may have been trying for *concatenation* – another good woid.

Cacophony has horribly illustrated the Gresham, or BIGO principle: it's now being used with comparative frequency, and almost invariably by people who should know better. An instructor at

Ryerson Polytech also cacaphonied on a CBC interview. Did he hear the folk-singer, and think to himself "Wow, that's Classy!" or what? How do these things spread so quickly? Another Classyist got the meaning right, but not the pronunciation: he made it kakaPHONy. Correct pronunciation: Ka-KOFF-on-y.

Chastise: Classy for criticize. "Michael Wilson's budget was chastised by all parties." I suspect they criticized it; why not say criticize? Chastisement is much more severe than criticism; it suggests "punishment (esp. corporal); a thrashing; very strong discipline, correction, or censure". I hate Michael's budget as much as the next one, and have indulged in fantasies about chastising Michael, but the budget needs careful evaluation and criticism, not a scolding or thrashing. There is some crossing, in that both can be used to express the idea of censure, but they are far from synonymous. To say (as a TV newswriter did) that Bob Rae chastised Premier Peterson for his cowardice on the insurance issue is to suggest a most unseemly brawl at Queen's Park. If the reporter had said that Mr. Rae had criticized Mr. Peterson, there would be no such uncomfortable ambiguity.

To critique: Another Classyism for criticize. What on earth is wrong with poor old criticize, that it's been abandoned, and these undesirables substituted? Critique is a noun, not a verb. A critique is "an essay or article in criticism of a literary work; a review. The action or art of criticizing."

Cryptic: Classy for curt, brusque, cutting. "My wife was pretty cryptic about the time I got home last night." Cryptic really means secret or hidden, occult, mystic, buried as in a crypt. Why the Classy speakers have taken it over for this totally unrelated meaning, God only knows.

Demise: Coming into Classy use to indicate some sort of failure or fall from eminence. It is also used for an election loss: "The demise of John Sewell in Toronto politics." Actually it is a legal term associated with the transfer of property; a derived meaning is death or abdication. Why not look it up? It's really highly inappropriate in most of its popular uses.

Enormity: Classy for something large or challenging: "The enormity of taking on Bjorn Borg in tennis." Strunk and White say (*The Elements of Style*) that it is correctly used "only in the sense of 'monstrous wickedness'. Misleading, if not wrong, when used to express bigness." The *Shorter Oxford* defines it as ". . . monstrous wickedness, abnormality, irregularity – a crime, a monstrous offence; a deviation from normal standards or type, esp. moral or legal."

Exhaustive: A Classy acquaintance thought the title of my *Exhaustive Concordance of the Bible* was hilarious; she believed it meant that the poor old concordance was dead with fatigue. Exhaustive (of books) means that they are thoroughly comprehensive, omitting nothing, so that the subject is exhausted. I tried to explain, but (typically Classy) she didn't listen. Later she was heard describing an exhaustive walk she was obliged to take when her car ran out of gas.

Fortuitous: Classy for fortunate, lucky. "I had a terrible hangover but fortuitously I'm getting over it." And, "They had an exceptionally fortuitous marriage." It really means produced by chance –accidental, casual. It's possible to be fortuitously unfortunate: a fortuitous circumstance could change everything for the worse.

Grandiose: Grander than grand, from the Classy point of view, because it has those delicious extra syllables. "The reception for the Duke and Duchess was really grandiose," gushed a reporter; not a nice thing to say about Andy and Fergie. "Producing, or trying to produce, the impression of grandeur; pompous."

Hankering: – Classy speakers seem to think this means hunch. "I have a hankering that you'll like this film." Actually, it's a mild longing, or craving. "I've got a hankering for seafood."

Homogenous (*sic*) – Classy error for homogeneous, itself often an error for heterogeneous. "We're a very homogenous group," gushed a lady, and proceeded to describe the wide variety of people who belonged to it. There is such a word as homogenous, but it's a bit special: "applied to organs or parts of different organisms which show correspondence of structure due to derivation from a common ancestor." Then there's homogonous – "having similar reproductive organs; applied to flowers in which there is no difference in length in the stamens and pistils of different individuals." That's some group, whether homogenous or homogonous. *Homogeneous* means of the same kind throughout, while heterogeneous means "diverse in kind or nature; not homogeneous."

In passing, *homo* meaning "the same", as in homosexual, is pronounced with a short *o*; it's derived from a Greek root. The Latin *homo*, meaning man, has a long *o*.

Incident is being replaced by (Classy) *incidence*, which is not the same thing at all. An incident is an event, occurrence or action: everyone worries about the increase in violent incidents in the home. *Incidence* means a range of occurrences or actions (e.g., the incidence of disease in certain areas or conditions). Nevertheless, a group of teachers on CBC Radio's "Cross-Country Check-up" all referred to "incidences of classroom violence". Not one of them knew the difference between incident and incidence. One of them also kept talking about parents who "abrogated" responsibility for their children. Abrogate means *to repeal or cancel a law or custom*; he probably meant abdicate. All right, it's close, and he was on a live broadcast, where one can't correct one's errors; still no excuse. Another error in that broadcast was "diagnosises"; how could a teacher perpetrate such a monstrosity, and how can we expect her students to use good English if she sets such a bad example?

Inkling: Stupid, if not Classy, for inclination. "If you have an inkling to grow house-plants . . ." A real inkling gives you a hint, a slight intimation, a suspicion. Confused, I suspect, with hankering.

Livid: Classy for . . . I don't know what. Since he called it livid, I simply couldn't figure out what he meant. "Livid stories", said someone on CBC's early morning show. But livid means "of a bluish leaden colour; discoloured as by a bruise; black and blue." I've noticed it creeping in when something like disturbing or distressing seems to be intended. This is the real objection to Classy language; it simply fails to communicate meaning. What is a bluish leaden-coloured story?

Literally: Classy speakers, out of pure perversity, have given this its diametrically opposite meaning. They use it when they mean metaphorically. Apropos of a fight in a bar, "This guy literally tore the place apart." What he actually did was break some glasses. The author of a book on aspirin, interviewed on "Gabereau", described how ". . . Tylenol came along, and literally blew them out of the water." Literally? What were the aspirin-manufacturers doing in the water, and what explosive did Tylenol use? And shouldn't a journalist and author know the difference between literally and metaphorically? A similar problem has arisen in connection with literacy and illiteracy, which many Classy speakers have difficulty in distinguishing. "The kinda teachers we had in high school, you can't blame us if we're literate," protested a Community College ornament.

Believe me, no one was about to accuse her of excessive literacy.

Massive: Classy for numerous, frequent, costly. "He paid massive amounts for her diamond." "I was massively tired." But massive (obviously) has to do with *mass*: compact, dense, existing in compact continuous masses.

Momento: Classy for memento, as in "I'd like you to have this little momento of your visit." Well, I don't want any momentos, see? I will, however, settle for a small memento. The correct form can easily be reMEMbered if you know that a MEMento is something to stimulate your MEMory. This has got tangled up with momentum, which is totally irrelevant in this context, since it means impetus gained by movement – "The avalanche was gathering momentum."

Nauseous: Classy for nauseated. "It was so ugly it made me nauseous." Or even, in some cases, "That guy makes me nauseous." (Usually pronounced nawshus.) I hope it, or he, didn't really make you nauseous, because that means you became loathesome, disgusting, highly offensive; unpleasant to the taste or smell; causing nausea or squeamishness". Now – are you really nauseous? Say it isn't so!

Odiferous: Classy for God knows what. Perhaps odoriferous, meaning diffusing scent or fragrance? Unknown to dictionaries, it occurred in a sub-head in a theatre review in the *Globe and Mail* by Ray Conlogue: "Odiferous Macho makes theatrical sense." Used twice. Where the hell are the editors? Does no one check this stuff?

Parameters: Classy for perimeters, or boundaries. It was a top favourite Classyism in the Seventies, usually in combination with viable. If you look up parameters, you'll find it means something so complicated that you can't possibly work it into any ordinary conversation. I'll spare you its mathematical, astronomical, and crystallographic applications, because its significance in general use (*gen.*) is disconcerting enough:

> A quantity which is constant (as distinct from the ordinary variables) in a particular case considered, but which varies in different cases; esp., a constant occurring in the equation of a curve or surface, by the variation of which the equation is made to represent a family of such curves or surfaces.

You call that viable?

Paranoid, Paranoiac: Classy for all sorts of inappropriate things. "I'm really getting paranoiac about these politicians who make a lot of promises and then forget about them till the next election." "That

Yolanda Ballard makes me so paranoid!" The *Encyclopaedia Britannica* says that the term paranoia is reserved for rare extreme cases of chronic fixed and highly systematized delusions. Paranoid states are less severe, although they are characterized by persistent delusions and by behaviour and emotional responses that are consistent with delusional ideas. Does Yolanda Ballard really do this to you?

In passing, a story in the Toronto *Star* (23 July 1988, p.A8) on the dangers of steroid use listed (conspicuously, in a box, to attract maximum attention) *Parnoid dillusions*. What kind of reporter could perpetrate that? What kind of editor could let it get into print? Makes me parnoid just to think of him collecting his pay cheque.

Poetaster: A friend sent me a clipping in which columnist/ broadcaster Arthur Black referred to Samuel Taylor Coleridge (aka Coalridge) as a "poetaster". He's calling the author of "The Ancient Mariner" and "Kubla Khan" *a paltry, inferior writer.* Could he really have meant that? I'll bet he thought it sounded (again, with mild facetiousness) rather Classy.

Pretentious, Portentous: Classy for excellent, impressive. There's no such word as portentious – they're trying for portentous. Both pretentious and portentous are insulting words, but the Classy speakers think they must be complimentary because of all those syllables. Pretentious means showy, ostentatious, making claim to importance which is not deserved. Portentous – of the nature of a portent, ominous, threatening, warning. It has come to have the meaning of pretentiousness – a portentous manner suggests great importance: "I am Sir Oracle, and when I ope my lips let no dog bark." It sometimes had a non-pejorative meaning, significant omen, in the past, but is not currently so used, except in Classy circles.

Prolific: "He's a prolific reader," says a CBC guest. "California is the most prolific user of water," says *Greenpeace*, August '89. Impossible, in both cases. If you're prolific, you're a producer, not a consumer. It means "generating or producing offspring; abundantly productive, fertilizing." Why not say that the man reads widely; that California uses large quantities of water? Because they think prolific sounds big time, uptown, Classy.

Prone, Supine: "The only position for a woman is prone." Pronouncement of a male chauvinist pig. The intention was to degrade women, suggesting their only function was as sex objects – to be tolerated only when they're lying on their backs. So he said the opposite, the big stupe, because *prone* means lying on your face. The word he was trying for was *supine*, but he didn't know what either word meant.

Shambles: "After Ben Johnson's disgrace, the Canadian sports scene was in shambles." Dear me, that's very serious indeed. Was it really in a slaughter-house, a place of carnage and wholesale slaughter, a place of blood? I can believe that it was very seriously upset, disorganized, disturbed. But wholesale slaughter is a bit thick, even when it's used metaphorically. "Nicaragua's economy is in shambles," said the six o'clock news on February 22nd, 1990. There's been plenty of blood in Nicaragua, but it's human, not economic. The economy is in crisis, though, because of the Contra war and the blockade imposed by the U.S.

Skittish: "Consumers are skittish about bio-engineered food." Skittish, when used of a horse, means "nervous, inclined to shy, excitable, playful, fidgety; of people (esp. women) says the *Shorter Oxford*, "frivolous, coquettish, excessively lively." I suspect that he intended sceptical, or possibly suspicious, or wary. The horse meaning could just be stretched to fit, but not the human. In the same broadcast ("The Food Show," CBC, October 14/90) they talked about someone "scarfing down" great quantities of food. The verb *to scarf* is used appropriately in carpentry, shipbuilding, and metalwork. He was trying for *scoff*: to eat greedily – possibly even avidly; it's slang, not to be confused with the other scoff, which means to deride, mock, or jeer.

Tortuous, Torturous: Classy for tortured. Great confusion here; tortuous means twisted, crooked, devious, as in "tortuous reasoning." Torturous means full of, involving, or causing torture. "Torturous prose" (Mary Langille, book review, Toronto *Star*) doesn't make much sense. She might have meant tortured, in the sense that it was "strained, twisted, or distorted," but neither torturous nor tortuous are applicable to a prose style.

Wreck Havoc: They're trying for *wreak havoc*. You can't really wreck havoc; it's a wrecker, not a wreckee. What you're saying is that you're destroying devastation, destruction, or disorder. Be nice if we could, but that wasn't the intent. To wreak havoc is (in this context) to inflict destruction on someone or something. You can also wreak revenge, and other disagreeable things.

Talking and/or Writing Classy is a filthy habit. It degrades the language, and makes its practitioners look stupid. If you have the choice of a simple, familiar word and a big fancy-sounding unfamiliar one, you should choose the simple and familiar every time. *Cultivate simplicity.*

Writers, editors and broadcasters must take responsibility for the correct use of language. How can teachers persuade students that good English is important, if the *Star* pays people to write about Parnoid Dillusions?

7

Lost Words
and Losing Battles

Our language is being impoverished in an unanticipated way –
unanticipated by me, in any case. We are losing words. Good
words, essential words, are simply being abandoned. Among these
casualties are the plural forms of the verb *to be*. Admittedly, it's faulty
and irregular, but that's no excuse for the abuse it's taking.

Remember (a few chapters ago) those five people who was injured in traffic accidents during a storm? They were also victims of
bad grammar: the current denial of a plural subject of its right to be
accompanied by a plural verb. Those five people WERE injured.
Subjects and verbs must agree in number. We have to restore "are"
and "were" to their rightful roles. Otherwise we'll soon be hearing
such intolerable locutions as "we is" and "they was": we *do* hear
them now, but they're still considered unacceptable. Why are they
any worse than "Five people was . . ."?

Not a day passes without someone in the media violating this fundamental grammatical law. "Running things are Gordon Walker,"
said Larry Zolf one morning. That would have been all right if Gordon had been assisted by a few others: "Running things are Gord
Walker, Bill Brewer, Jan Stewer, Peter Gurney . . ." But no. Lonely
Gordon were running it all by himself. A few minutes later, Mr. Zolf
added– in another context– "There has been some changes made."
Has is singular, *changes* plural. It won't do! "There *have* been some
changes made." At least one more should be made, if Larry doesn't
check out subject-verb agreement.

There is/ There are; There was/ There were. In these constructions, the plural seems to have been discarded completely. "There is two different philosophies," said actress Jackie Burroughs during a CBC interview, and proceeded to discourse learnedly about philosophies of theatre production. Surely these people know the difference between singular and plural? *is* and *are?* There is one, there ARE two. Do they really not know any better, or is it just a slovenly habit? People in theatre, as well as people in broadcasting, have a responsibility to the public. They should set a good example. How many impressionable children might be influenced by your sloppy English, ever think of that? "There is many people today that are willing to make sacrifices for the environment." An admirable sentiment, abominably phrased. Obviously, there ARE many such people. But not people *that.* People are *who*, another word that is disappearing from the language. Who, that, and which are surrounded by controversy; I'll come back to this shortly.

"There is patterns of changing behaviour . . ." That was yet another academic, in an interview. How can we expect kids to use good English if their instructors don't bother? "If gold ruste, what shal iren do?" That's Chaucer, not a mistake in spelling.

As noted, we're losing the verb *are* in constructions like "there are", and the conjunction *who* in relative clauses; we're also losing a variety of useful words because their roles have been usurped by less desirable ones. For example, *persuade* has been almost entirely supplanted by *convince*, which doesn't mean the same thing. "I'm gonna convince my boy-friend to take me to Florida in March break." In fact, she hoped to persuade him, by feminine arts. Convince means something much tougher: to overcome or vanquish. That "vince" comes from the Latin *vinco*, to conquer, defeat, vanquish. A Damon Runyon term for a gun was "the old convincer."

Furthermore, you convince someone OF something, not TO something.

Or you could convince him THAT it was unwise to abuse such a truculent verb. Still another lost word is *ignorant,* in its true sense of being unlearned, uninformed, lacking knowledge. It's now used to mean offensive or obnoxious. Perhaps this trend started with people being ignorant of proper behaviour, and so offensive or obnoxious: "These guys get kinda ignorant when they've had a few drinks." They really get kinda obnoxious, perhaps because of their ignorance of acceptable behaviour.

Lost: *fewer*. This essential word has been largely, and incorrectly, supplanted by *less*. *Questions You've Always* etc. has an invaluable little mnemonic on this, which I will steal (but will request permission to use, honest):

> Don't settle for *less* where the sense calls for *fewer*, and it calls for *fewer* if the noun following it is in the plural (e.g. *less bread, fewer rolls; less time, fewer days*...) When considering words of quantity, here's an easy rule: *little money, few dollars; much money, many dollars; less money, fewer dollars*. Where a unit of time or money is involved, *less* may be used: He had *less* than ten dollars with him; he had served *less* than ten years. BUT *Fewer* troops in Southeast Asia means *less* money spent on the military. (p. 72)

There have been complaints to CBC from listeners and readers about the abandonment of *fewer*, and the misuse of *less*. Unfortunately, a parallel to the *like/as* confusion has resulted. They simply started using *fewer* where they should use *less*. Professor Robert Picard, editor of the *Journal of Media Economics* was talking about "fewer and fewer money" on "Media File", July 22, 1989. Even making allowances for unrehearsed speech, on a live broadcast, it's difficult to forgive anything as dreadful as this. How can they face themselves? If gold ruste . . .

Also lost is understanding of comparatives and superlatives. A public school grammar book had an exercise specifically intended to train people out of using double comparatives. How can we restore it to the curriculum? Hardly a day passes when we are spared such atrocities as "more better" or "more faster."

"Science faculties have always believed that women are less better than men," said a woman professor ("Morningside" again). Please – no double comparatives, especially when they contradict one another. This lady teaches in a science department, but science students need to hear literate English from their instructors as much as anyone else. How can anything be less better? Women students might (unfairly) be judged as less competent in science, or less naturally inclined to study it. They could even be less good at it, in some cases, though it would be much better to say they had less aptitude, or inferior skill. But "less better" is idiotic.

On the same programme, a high school teacher (subject area unspecified, but I hope it wasn't English) described something as "more truer." One or the other, please. Double comparatives are odious.

Recently I heard someone discussing "the most number of murders" and "one of the most major problems" of contemporary society. Major is a comparative; you can't modify a comparative by a superlative. "The least worst" has now become commonplace; I've found it not only in periodicals, but in novels, one by a teacher of writing.

Another threatened word, believe it or not, is the simple indefinite article *a*. Remember *a?* Its disappearance isn't noticeable in spoken English, but in writing the article is being combined with other words: alot, alittle, abig. I suspect this is actually being *taught*, because students were clearly baffled when I marked it as an error. *Someone is teaching them to do this.* But *a* is a word in its own right, for all its small size, and is perfectly capable of standing by itself. It should not be mushed in with the next word, for a variety of reasons. Suppose, just for argument, that you wanted to look up *lot* in the dictionary, and you thought it was spelled *alot*. You'd never find it, and serve you right, too.

Lost: *talk*. Believe it or not, this indispensable word is threatened – not in all its uses, but far too frequently. "We gotta sit down and dialogue," I heard a lady say this morning. You could tell from her tone that this activity was a lot Classier than sitting down for a simple old talk. Actually, dialogue was once used as a verb but it is archaic, and now considered affected. Personally, I'd rather talk, or perhaps chat.

"Talk" is threatened from another direction, by the highly non-Classy but vogueish "go". It occurs mostly among teenagers, and those adults who aspire to be perennially young. "So he goes, 'You wanna go to the party with me tonight?' and she goes, 'No kidding?' and he goes, 'Yeah, sure,' and she goes . . ."

Yet another casualty is the verb *to turn*. No one who wants to be considered "in" or "with it" (whatever the current term may be) would be caught turning, or making a turn. You have to *hang*. I keep hearing it from my contemporaries, in a peculiar, self-congratulatory tone . . . I believe they think they sound dashing and contemporary when they say, "Hang a left at Mohawk, go two blocks, and when you come to Garth, hang another left . . ."

Why "hang", which loses all sense in the context, when what I have to do is make a left turn, in all that filthy traffic? Where does the hanging come in?

Lost: "I couldn't care less." This was a Second World War coinage, I believe, a not particularly inspired way of saying that you care nothing, and it's impossible to have less than nothing. For no evident reason, it became a great vogue. It has now been corrupted to "I could care less", which means exactly the opposite of what is intended. It means that you *do* care, since you're capable of caring less. All right, this is a pretty laborious explanation of a minor point, but I'm tired of hearing, "I could care less," often in rather superior tones, as if they were saying something clever – indeed, Classy. It's often on the lips of people who should know better, such as singer Anne Murray. I've heard that Anne was a school-teacher, in pre-Snowbird days. Now she's in a position to influence the speech habits of millions. Think, Anne!

Lost: *man*. This one needs some qualification. It is still used in certain contexts, often with a negative connotation; violent feminists have actually made the word itself into an abuse term. In other circles, it has been completely supplanted by the term "gennelman". This is now used almost exclusively in police circles, as in the report, "When his nose started to bleed, Mr. Jukes then kicked the other gennelman in the stummick."

Lost: *Miss* (courtesy term). This of course has been chiefly supplanted by Ms., and I'm not complaining. Theoretically, women and men are now referred to in newspaper stories by their last names, in the interest of equality, but in practice, there has been a total switch. I recently read (in I forget which paper) an account of a rape case in which the accused was referred to throughout as Mr. Smith, while his victim was never Miss Brown, or Mary Brown, but Brown, *tout court*. Well, serve her right – she probably wore enticing clothes, or danced in a provocative manner. As everyone knows, such behaviour is an unequivocal invitation to rape. She doesn't deserve to be called Miss, or Ms.

Lost: *exactly the same*, deplorably supplanted by *the exact same*. "Quibble, quibble, quibble," groaned one of my victim/critics. Well, I'm sorry. Although it now appears to be in universal use, I will nevertheless raise one faint cry of protest. *Same* can be a pronoun, an adjective, or an adverb; in this construction it seems to be an adjective, as in *the same dress, the same car*. However, *exact* is also an adjective, and adjectives can't modify adjectives; only adverbs can do that. So we need the adverbial form *exactly*. Since we are seeking the exactly right form, we can't for some reason or other (probably idiomatic) say, "the exactly same". *Exactly the same* seems to be the best we can do. "That was the exact same moccasin I was trying to describe to that jerk in the shoe store," complained Lolita, way back in the Fifties, of a shoe left by the roadside after a tragic accident. It was the first time I ever encountered this perversion. Now it's everywhere. Gresham's Law (BIGO) is remorseless.

To return to the lost *who* – it's not completely lost. It survives as an interrogative pronoun - "Who was that lady I seen you with?" [Antique joke]. It's almost completely lost in its role as a conjunction: "The engineer who built the bridge . . ." has become "The engineer that built the bridge." "The woman who inspired the character of Tess" has been demoted to a *that*. The original idea was that *who* was used of people (and sometimes of animals) while *that* was reserved for non-human creation. Pet dogs were often *who*, dinosaurs were *that*. Fowler's *English Usage* defends the use of *that* in certain cases, but other authorities reject it. My personal preference is for "who", when there's any question, partly because sentences often tend to get cluttered up with "thats".

There may be a contributing factor in the abandonment of *who* because of anxiety about whether (and when) it should be *whom*. Many people have great difficulties with whom, and have developed a phobia about its use. There is actually a society in the U.S. for the abolition of whom. However, there is a Classy element which considers whom to be somehow more refined or elegant than either who or that, introducing it at every possible, and many an impossible, occasion.

I'm ambivalent about whom. I usually know what's right, but sometimes what's right tends to sound stuffy, like "It is I". And then there's the Classy association, from which I prefer to disassociate myself. Remember Lily Tomlin's Ernestine, the telephone operator – a marvellously witty whom-user: "Is this the party that I'm connected to whom?" "To whom am I speaking to?" Ernestine, who was inclined to boast about her high school education, often worked in as many as three "whoms" in a sentence, making them sound so refined and genteel that the teeth of the anti-whom school were set on edge. "She makes me want to spit on the floor," said an admirer.

Ms Magazine had an editorial in its September/October issue, 1991, with the headline. "Who *Can* We Trust? Ourselves". Now that should be whom. It's the object of the verb trust. Perhaps this gives us a clue. In ordinary conversation, it seems quite natural to say, "Who can we trust?" But in a Page One headline of a major publication, perhaps we're justified in requiring a correct and formal whom.

A word whose loss I frequently regret is *aggravate*. It means to make worse, to exaggerate, to put weight upon, to add weight unduly. (That's metaphoric weight, not flab.) However, it's now generally used to mean to annoy, to irritate or, familiarly, to hassle. We have a good supply of words to express this, but aggravate was useful, if not indispensable. I'm afraid, however, that it is doomed to join unique in the great garbage heap of lost words and lost causes.

Endangered, if not yet lost, is *obstinacy*, which is being replaced, for no visible reason, by obstinance, a word unknown in dictionaries. (I checked five.) I found this in Linda McQuaig's brilliant *The Quick and the Dead*. Well, we all make mistakes, and Ms. McQuaig is a writer I admire just this side idolatry. But surely all those clever editors at Viking and Penguin should have caught it?

Endangered: *suspicious*, which is being replaced by *suspect*. "The natives [of Spadina Avenue] remain suspect of introducing street car service on the Avenue." If that was really what CBC intended (News, Nov. 6 1991), it would mean that the Spadina natives were possibly guilty of trying to get streetcar service. In fact, the opposite was the case: the natives opposed streetcars, and feared their effect on traffic. They were *suspicious* that someone was trying to push unwanted streetcars on them. They suspected this, but if they had been suspect, they would have been the suspected instead of the suspecting.

Another example of confusion with this word: "I'm suspect that Japan's foreign policy may be about to change drastically." Japan's foreign policy may be suspect, but the speaker is suspicious. For some inexplicable reason, suspect in this quite undesirable context is considered extremely classy.

CHAPTER

8

Redundancy and
Related Absurdities

If the Classy syndrome and an inadequate grounding in grammatical principles are the sources of the worst contemporary tooth-grinders, then redundancy comes close behind. It's curious that so many flaws in usage come from the unconscious belief that more is better.

Some examples: sufficient enough; over-exaggerate; other alternative; often-times; surrounding environs. If you have sufficient, you by definition have enough. If you exaggerate, you are over-stating. If you have an alternative, it is literally "other": *alter* is Latin for other. Often means "many times, frequently." If you insist on saying often-times, and thousands are so insisting, you're saying "many times-times" or "frequently times." Your environs are, literally, your surroundings, so that you're saying "surrounding surroundings." Do they never think about what words *mean*? Why say everything twice?

"Meet up with" – a few years ago it was a comic vulgarism. Now Gresham's Law has taken over, and it is rotting away at the language everywhere. If you meet someone, you meet them. What is added by sticking in a totally useless up, and with? Mystery writer Amanda Cross, who makes much of her intellectual and academic superiority, incessantly commits this vulgar redundancy.

"In my opinion, I don't believe . . ." If that's your opinion, you've already stated your belief/disbelief. Why say it twice?

"I have a friend of mine that says . . ." You have a friend who says, *or* A friend of yours says . . . Why do you need them both?

"A great deal amount of money was invested . . ." Oh, for heaven's sake! This is a special variety of redundancy (we call it syntactical redundancy in the trade) in which two constructions are unnecessarily involved. You can either say "A great deal of money" or "a large amount of money" but for pity's sake, how can you have a "great deal amount"? And the financial authority who perpetrated this horror said it twice. It wasn't just a stumble.

Free gifts and true facts have been with us for a long time, but that doesn't make them desirable. Obviously if you give someone a gift it's free; if you charge for it, it isn't a gift. Similarly, there's no such thing as an untrue fact. If it isn't true, it isn't a fact. Nor are cheap prices much of a bargain. Cheap means low-priced. The thing on sale may be cheap, in which case its price is low; a cheap price is a low-price price. And speaking of prices – or non-prices – nothing is "for free." It's simply free. This was once used facetiously (cf from whence) but it has now percolated into general usage.

"Thusly": Aaagghhhh. The suffix "ly" means "in such a fashion or degree". That's also what "thus" means, so that you're saying "thus thus". A caller on CBC's "As It Happens" was discussing nude bathing: "Do I want people thusly clad on the beach?" Naked people are unclad, not clad, and thusly is inexcusable. His tone communicated that he was pleased with his dreadful phrase: it sounded Classy!

You understand that none of these categories have been given exhaustive treatment; these are mere samplings.

The next examples are not redundancies in the pure sense, like "other alternatives"; perhaps they might be described as padding, or stuffing. These are words that have nothing much to do with what you're saying, but are stuffed in without thought. Frequently, unfortunately, there's a Classy element involved. *Basically*, for example was considered a very impressive, uptown word a few years ago. It has lost its chic from over-use, and now has simply become a bad habit, along with *y'know*, and *like*. They are often used unconsciously, but they can be very tiresome for the listener. Gore Vidal has a story about the compulsive inclusion of "like" in every phrase: a drowning hippy was supposed to have called out, "Like, help!"

"Y'know" is a disease among pop singers and rock musicians, many of whom are incapable of a sentence in which "y'know" doesn't occur at least five times.

"Basically, it's based on four basic rules." I didn't make that up. I still have difficulty believing that it actually issued from the mouth of an allegedly educated person – a teacher of some description. He was explaining, in a CBC interview, a sadistic device called the "discipline box". I'd like to put him in his box, until he swears off "basically".

A few more samples: *co-operating together*. Co-operating is working together. *Continued on* – no *on*. If you continue, you are going on or keeping on. *3:30 a.m. in the morning*. If it's a.m., it has to be morning. *Rise up* – you can't rise down. *More preferable* – If it's preferable, you like it more, by definition. *Following after* – How could you follow anywhere else? Let's see you follow before.

The addition of unnecessary words has become a disease of the language. Consider *to it*. "Her hair had a beautiful sheen to it." Take out that ugly and unnecessary *to it* and her hair still has its beautiful sheen. *As of* – "She was holding her own as of two weeks before." But wasn't she holding her own two weeks before, without that silly *as of*? *Get hold of* or, worse, *Get ahold of*: all you need is *get*. "He wanted to get ahold of enough information to write the report." If he gets enough information, he can write the report without any horrid *ahold of*. Let us not forget *off of*, as in "He fell off of his horse." If he fell off, the wretched creature was off – a perfectly good preposition that has no need for the support of an unnecessary *of*.

Do some of these examples sound improbable? I haven't invented a single one. The samples in the last two paragraphs all came from published books, some of them by novelists who give themselves airs about their superior literacy. And no editor corrected them.

9

Prepositions, Pronouns, and Other Booby-traps

The vexed and vexing question of prepositions was touched on in an earlier chapter, apropos of "like I said". I won't try to define a preposition, since I've just looked it up in the dictionary and the definition is so confusing that I wish I hadn't bothered. Instead I'll give you some examples: in, on, of, at, over, under, with . . . that'll do for a start. Little ordinary words that introduce phrases.

Prepositions are harmless as long as their object is a noun. "There's a fly in my soup." (Grammatically harmless, not gastronomically.) *In* is the preposition, *soup* is its object. The trouble starts when the object is a pronoun – one of those little stand-ins for nouns, which have the inconvenient habit of varying in form, depending on their grammatical function. That is, *he* is subjective, *him* objective. All this will be insultingly obvious to people with some knowledge of grammar, but believe me, folks, you're a minority. The majority, which includes many university graduates, hasn't the foggiest notion of what either a preposition or a pronoun may be. All I ask you to remember is that when a pronoun follows a preposition, it should be in the objective case, as in, "Come with me to the Casbah." Not "Come with I." *I* subject, *me* object. No trouble so far; wait for it.

Rose Macaulay gives a nice illustration of how it goes wrong in *The Towers of Trebizond*, in which her mother invites her to "go to Cyprus, with Howard and I."

My mother is not common, but she has never been able to grasp grammar, or why it is wrong to talk about flying to Cyprus with I. She did not say "flying with I", but if anyone else was flying too, she thought that this put the first person singular into the nominative case, and that this was a rule of grammar.

Rose's mum has plenty of company.

"It's incumbent on we in the media to use good English," I actually heard someone say on radio a few days ago. Would she have said, "It's incumbent on we to use good English"?

"They put all the responsibility on she and I," complained a lady in an interview. On we?

"The whole community turned out to give support for he and his family," advised CBC reporter Heather Evans. For they?

The errors tend to occur with a compound object, or when a qualifier of some sort – "in the media" – is involved. Surely no one would put all the responsibility on we? Nor would the community have turned out to support they. I trust Ms. Evans would not say "for he"; then why change it because of the addition of "and his family"?

"Between you and I" is of course a longstanding example. I've been sternly corrected when I insisted on saying "between you and me". Interestingly, "between you and I" is considered Classy: somehow, *I* has come to be considered more elegant than *me*.

Now if one has assimilated the grammatical rules, and learned the subjective and objective cases of pronouns, and how they are used with verbs and prepositions, one simply cannot make these foolish errors. Unfortunately, a good many people seem to have got through school without so much as hearing of their existence.

Just for the record: It's incumbent on us in the media (or out of it) to use good English. The responsibility falls on us, that is, *on her and me*. *She and I* can't be us – they're we. And although the community should not, in the interest of good grammar, turn out for he, it should come out cheering to give support *for him and his family*.

A related pronoun error occurs in another grammatical structure, with subjects/objects of verbs. Columnist John Vince wrote in the Hamilton *Spectator*, "It is the dependency ratio that has we retirement planners worried." It has we worried? Recently a playwright and producer for the Edmonton Fringe Theatre spoke at length about his passion for language and literature, and then described his collaboration with another writer. "Him and I worked together on several productions." Mercy. How can you say a thing like that, if you have so much respect for language?

A few years ago, such a gaffe would have marked you as educationally underprivileged. Now it's almost standard English. Kelly Crowe, an up-and-coming young TV journalist, reporting on the Barbara Dodd case, advised that "Her and her boy-friend then left the press conference." This on network news. Isn't it rather embarrassing to expose such a dubious level of literacy to the listening world? And a sports reporter, talking of skater Brian Orser, claimed that ". . . him and the other Brian, although rivals, are good friends."

Prepositions, by their nature, are supposed to introduce a phrase: *prepone*, Lat., to put before. They always do in Latin, because of the way the language works, and so (concluded the pedants) they must always do it in English, too. This has led to some strange and monstrous practices, since English doesn't always work the same way as Latin.

Students were taught that they must NEVER end a sentence with a preposition. Teachers spent weary hours trying to make their victims say "with whom" and "in which", to avoid the terminal preposition. The result has been more, and worse, grammatical atrocities than the one they're trying to avoid. Imperfectly assimilated, the rule led to the dread "in which" syndrome: some students decided that the two words are inseparable, regardless of sense or meaning.

"Women should get the credit in which they deserve." "The idea in which Barbara Amiel is trying to get across . . ." "My personal experiences, in which have been many, I feel closely revolve around the realm of the supernatural."

In passing: there's something about the supernatural that brings out the worst kind of grammar and English use. I once taught a course dealing with the supernatural in literature, and it produced the worst spelling – the worst everything – I encountered in all my years of teaching. My colleagues (hardened though they were to student errors) used to accuse me of making them up. I *couldn't* have made them up. End of digression. Back to prepositions and pronouns.

On another CBC programme ("Later the Same Day") the host invited listener participation to discuss the question, "How would you describe the person with whom you most like to be with?" Ordinary common sense gets lost and grammatical lunacy ensues.

The absurdity of the banning of the terminal preposition was illustrated by Winston Churchill (in ironic response to a pompous memo from a pedantic civil servant) with the Horrible Example, "up with which I will not put" instead of the normal and natural sequence of "which I won't put up with."

Fowler says: "Follow no arbitrary rule . . . If the final preposition that has naturally presented itself sounds comfortable, keep it; if it does not sound comfortable, still keep it if it has compensating vigour, or when among awkward possibilities it is the least awkward."

Preposition abuse has become epidemic in recent years. People have been saying (correctly) for years, "The secret of his success . . ." Recently, for no intelligible reason, abusers have changed that perfectly sound "of" to the inappropriate "to." "The secret to his success . . ."

A newspaper food editor offered suggestions in her column for people "who are bored to chicken salad."

Almost universal is the hideous "sick to my stomach". This used to be another of those hallmark phrases which I can only classify, at the risk of sounding like a snob, as "underprivileged" or "lower-class." Why *to?* Why is it necessary to specify the physiology? If you're talking to the doctor, you can say, "My stomach is upset," or "I'm having a digestive upset." In general conversation, the topic should simply be avoided. Or if it *can't* be avoided, for desperate reasons, you can say, "Excuse me – where is the bathroom?" Or even, "Look out! I'm going to be sick!" We don't need to know where you're going to be sick to, at, or in. Spare us. Go away and get it over with, in private.

To seems to be constantly muscling in where it has no right to be. Oddly enough, it has been long lost where it's actually needed. "I'm gonna try and get a new car." Or ominously, "If I get good enough marks, I'm gonna try and get into U. of T." If you're trying to do something, you're not trying *and* it. Try to correct this bad habit, please!

These may seem like small matters, but as you can see, they are contributing to the erosion of the language. Precision and clarity get lost in the fog of small, slovenly errors that obscure effective communication.

CHAPTER

10

Confusion Worse Confounded

English is rich in pairs or sets of words which can easily be confused. When in doubt, avoid them until you can check a dictionary. For some perverse reason, the inept word-user unerringly chooses the wrong one. Here's my personal collection:

Ambiguous/ambivalent: Ambiguous means having a double meaning, being capable of more than one meaning. Ambivalent emotions are contradictory; you feel both love and hate, or other opposed feelings, toward the same object or person. You can't, therefore, feel ambiguous about him/her. You can, however, have ambivalent feelings for the unfortunate wretch, and until you get them clarified, it would be most unwise to commit yourself to anything serious, or spend a lot of money on diamonds. Ambivalent (accent on the BIV) is a very recently coined word; psychologists invented (or coined) it, to describe the conflicting emotions they were discovering in patients and even in themselves. I looked in three dictionaries before I could find one that acknowledged its existence, though I've been using it for years. Dictionaries are often slow to catch up with usage. Still condemned in purist circles as a neologism, ambivalent has come into general use, and is indispensable.

Biography/Autobiography: Now this one seems so easy and obvious that you'd wonder how anyone could confuse them. Stop wondering: lots of people can and do. A biography is the history of the life of an individual, written by someone else. An autobiography is your life-story, related by you. That *auto* prefix means "of or by oneself". Thus, an automobile is something that moves by itself. Seems obvious, but a CBC reporter from Newfoundland described an entertainer who related his own biography to the audience. The same reporter several times referred to thee*air*ical experience and life in the thee-aiter. Couldn't believe my ears.

Shouldn't there be some sort of test for these people, before they're turned loose on the public with a microphone?

Censor/censure/censer/sensor: The censor (whose job is to censor and sometimes to censure as well) inspects books, plays, films, and so on, to ensure that they contain "nothing immoral, heretical, or offensive or injurious to the state". To censure means to reprimand, to make an adverse judgement, to express disapproval. You can get a job (if you're qualified) as a censor, but not as a censure, which is a condemnation or expression of disapproval. Censers play a minor role in English usage, unless you're a dedicated church-goer, but they contribute to the confusion: a censer is a vessel for burning incense. A sensor, however, detects or measures physical properties to which it is responsive or sensitized. Science students should be aware of it, and of how to distinguish it from censors and censers.

Complement/compliment: This is a written-word error, since you can't tell the difference in spoken language. Most of the written word producers are unaware of the existence of "complement", and make poor old "compliment" do the work of two, although their confusion about the meaning often betrays itself in the context. To complement is to fulfil, or complete, or make perfect. "Her accessories complemented her dress." Fashion writers adore complement, which they invariably spell as if it were "a flattering expression, formal congratulation, or mark of courtesy". I believe they think it means that the accessories, in harmonizing with the dress, are paying it a nice little tribute.

Contemptible/contemptuous: If something is contemptible, it's deserving of contempt. If someone is contemptuous, he's feeling contempt for something contemptible. I am contemptuous of Classy speakers/writers, who have the contemptible habit of misusing language.

Credulous/credible, with which we might as well include *incredulous/incredible.* If you're credulous, you'll swallow anything; you're gullible, or too ready to believe. If you're incredulous, you're the reverse – unwilling to believe. If something is credible, it's believable, convincing, worthy of belief. Incredible: unbelievable, unconvincing. Now used near-universally to mean large or expensive: "He drives this incredible BMW." *Creditable*, on the other hand, is used in a complimentary sense – if your conduct is creditable, it does you credit. You're great! *Credence* means belief: if you give credence to something, you believe it. But it is increasingly misused for credibility.

Disinterested/uninterested: Generally, the whole world (not only Classyists) uses disinterested when they mean uninterested. When they want to express true disinterestedness, they're in trouble. The closest synonym is impartial, not influenced by one's own advantage. Unbiased judges should be disinterested, for example, but should be fired if they're uninterested.

Flaunt/flout: For some unfathomable reason, almost no one seems able to get these two straight. I know a Ph.D. in Philosophy who still flaunts traffic regulations – an irresponsible act, both practically and linguistically. Kathryn Brink, a columnist in the Hamilton *Spectator* deplores the situation when a child "flaunts the moral expectations of parents". I know this is an exercise in futility but let's try anyway. To flaunt is to wave proudly; to make a show or display of; to show off, or parade oneself or one's finery. To flout is to mock, scoff at, insult, defy or express contempt for something. Flout has almost disappeared from the language, as everybody flaunts laws, rules, traditions, etc., while flaunt is in danger of dying from overwork.

Imply/infer: Another hopeless case, but we must not flag nor fail. Fighting on to the end, we learn that imply means to insinuate or hint at the truth or existence of a thing without expressly asserting it. Following such an implication, you infer, or draw an inference, you deduce or conclude that the speaker means something that he hasn't the guts to come right out with. Among the uninstructed, infer is chronically used for imply; implications are too subtle for them altogether. "Are you inferring that I'm ignorant?" Yes, dear.

Lose/loose: Everyone knows what these mean, but there is a tendency to dump lose (pronounced looz), meaning to be unable to find something, and to use loose (rhymes with goose) everywhere. Loose can be adjective, adverb, and verb. You can lose your wallet, but you wear loose-fitting clothes; you can lose your dog, or you can loose him from his chain, which sometimes produces the same result.

Mitigate/militate: "President Reagan's policies mitigated against a quick solution to the arms race." CBC again. They're fumbling for *militate*, meaning to work against, fight against, be directed against. Militate is always followed by *against.* The words look something alike, but their meanings are almost opposite. President Reagan's policies did indeed militate against a quick solution to the arms race, but the arrival on the international scene of Mr. Gorbachev had a mitigating effect: that is, moderating or mollifying. To mitigate a punishment is to make it less severe.

Reticent/reluctant: Oh dear. Even the literate seem to have difficulty with these, although it's quite unnecessary. Reticence is reserve *in speech*, avoidance of saying all one knows or feels, or more than is necessary; disposition to silence, taciturnity. (Which, in passing is not pronounced with a *k.*) In some respects, therefore, it is akin to reluctant. The reticent person is reluctant to do a lot of talking, to tell you anything, in fact. However, the two are by no means synonymous. Some people are reluctant to keep their traps shut; they monopolize conversations and bore you frantic. You wish they would be more reticent. To be reluctant is to be unwilling, disinclined to do something. One does not, therefore, speak of being "reticent to speak": you're reluctant to speak. If you're reticent, it by definition affects speech. However, you DON'T say, "I was reticent about going in the water, because it was pretty cold." You were reluctant, you sissy!

Voracious/Vociferous: These polysyllables have great Classy appeal but are frequently confused, with unfortunate results. CBC's Denise Rudnicki spoke of "voracious critics" in reviewing a book called *Somebody Owes Me Money.* Another CBC reporter, whose name I failed to catch, was discussing a plague of tent caterpillars which, she said, were eating vociferously. Susan Cardinal, of CBC's "Sunday Morning", spoke of "voracious complaints about the GST."

Dictionary, please, ladies. Voracious means gluttonous, ravenous, greedy – avid, even! Vociferous, however, means clamorous, bawling, noisy. Much as I dislike tent caterpillars, this is one fault of which they can't be fairly accused.

This list is by no means complete; there are dozens of other look-alike sound-alike words in English, and it must be admitted that they're confusing. It's easy to make a slip, especially (for example) on a live, unrehearsed broadcast. Nevertheless, if words are your business, you have an obligation to use them accurately and correctly. If you've taken the trouble to learn the difference between reticent and reluctant, you're unlikely to mix them up, even under stressful conditions.

No one expects a crane-operator or a cab-driver to be as meticulous about language as an English teacher, but if you've undertaken a profession that deals in words, you should be prepared to master the tools of the trade. How would you like to be driven by a cabby who didn't know how to turn on his lights, or shift from park into reverse?

And now for homework: using the dictionary, distinguish between continual/continuous, past/passed, affect/effect, exasperate/exacerbate. Marks will be deducted for spelling errors.

11

Spelling Bee

"*I* can't spell!"

They giggle and snigger after making this admission, as if they were confessing to something adorable and fetching. Aren't I the cute, naughty little thing, though! There is a suggestion in their admission that ability to spell is boring and pedestrian (like being a good housekeeper), while bad spelling is a sign of creativity and originality.

"I guess I'm just too artistic to be a good speller," laughed one of these darlings.

Aptitude for spelling varies, and sometimes it seems almost as if there were a spelling gene, an instinct, which makes it easy and natural for some people, difficult for others.

Bad spelling is therefore forgivable, with the proviso that the deprived person is willing to work at it. It is unforgivable, though, in teachers, writers (including journalists), editors, librarians, and others who set up as mentors to the impressionable young. Spelling can be *learned*, and if you want to be a role model, you have an obligation to work at it, humbly and continually. You have no right to pass on your bad habits and your ignorance to the people you're supposed to be instructing.

CBC'S "Radio Noon" once held a spelling bee, enlisting the help of a head librarian from a North York library. I should give her name, because she should have been a good deal more ashamed of herself than she was, but somehow I can't bring myself to do it. She admitted that she wasn't a Grade A speller, but she didn't admit that she was downright rotten. Why did she agree to conduct a spelling match, when she must have known she was bad at it? And why didn't CBC take the trouble to ensure that they had someone of proven ability? Perhaps they didn't know how?

The spelling "expert" challenged the listeners to spell her choice of words, after which the listeners could challenge the alleged expert. One of the words the Top Librarian asked listeners to spell was "ebbyulent", by which she intended "ebullient", which should be pronounced *e-BULL-yent*, accent on the bull. Now if you're a top class librarian in a big city library, with lots of dictionaries available for consultation, you have absolutely no excuse for not knowing how to pronounce words. And if you're going to conduct a spelling match on network radio, you damn well have a responsibility to make sure you're pronouncing the words correctly.

Moreover, this lady made a great many spelling errors herself, on national radio. She put two l's in broccoli, and was not corrected; she mis-spelled septuagenarian and Brobdingnagian. Neither she nor the radio host knew what either word meant, and excused themselves on the latter by saying that proper names weren't allowed.

How can you get through university to become a top librarian or host of a big radio show without reading *Gulliver's Travels?* Brobdingnag was the giants' country, and the adjective Brobding-nagian has become part of the language, to describe anything enormous, just as Lilliputian is used for something extremely small.

It was a very distressing programme. Surely it's ominous, not only that the education system is turning out people with such low skills and placing them in responsible positions, but that the people themselves seem contented with such low standards, and display no embarrassment or concern for their poor performance?

We all make mistakes; no one is infallible. I found, during the spelling bee, that I'd been misspelling ukulele all my life. I could have forgiven her an error or two. But not to look up the pronunciation of the words she was using; to make repeated spelling mistakes, and then try to defend them ("Proper names aren't allowed"); not even to recognize a name from *Gulliver* – haven't we a right to expect more from a head librarian?

Teaching spelling is no joke, and English is a famously inconsistent language. The old system relied entirely on phonetics, on "sounding-out" words – which demonstrated its inadequacy as soon as you struck words like cough, and rough, and sough. In view of this difficulty, a group of reformers in the Fifties decided spelling should be taught by word-recognition, a method that had certain advantages, and that often worked for people with good visual memories.

It didn't work at all for many other people, and it produced generations of students who couldn't tell the difference between television, telephone, and telemarketing: they recognized the first syllable and guessed the balance. This produced dreadful results in reading skills and comprehension.

The word-recognition boys could produce compelling arguments for their method, but the fact is that it didn't work any better than (in fact not as well as) phonetics. Obviously, we need them both. But the word-recognizers refused to tolerate the existence of sounding-out – it had to be banished absolutely. It took years for them to realize that their system wasn't working either, and still more years for them to concede the fact. They were years that produced generations of hopelessly incompetent spellers and readers.

As a friend has pointed out to me, those of us who learned to "sound" can usually figure out the meaning and pronunciation of words we've never seen before, even if we're not pronouncing them perfectly. Those who learned only word-recognition have no hope; they might as well be looking at Chinese symbols.

At this point in the argument, someone invariably introduces the word "ghoti" which is an alternative spelling for fish. Gh as in laugh, o as in women, ti as in adventitious or repetitious. (Actually, it's the itious which gives the "sh" sound, not the ti, but let it go.)

Let's face it: some things – the alphabet, the multiplication table, the spelling of certain words – just have to be memorized. But oddly enough, the very people who champion word recognition have a grudge against memorization, and want to banish it, with the result that generations have grown up with no memory-store of poetry, and that's a pity.

The current system is not to teach spelling at all in early grades. They've gone back to sounds, with a vengeance; the children write everything exactly as it occurs to them (write becomes rit, head is hed). The object of this is to avoid discouraging creativity. Back to the Sixties: as long as they can express their feelings, nothing else matters.

It's the same principle that dominates the teaching of art: let them slap down anything they want, forget techniques, just as long as they're creative, as long as they're expressing themselves. It may work at kindergarten level, but at some point there has to be recognition of the need for technique, discipline, craftsmanship.

According to a music teacher, the same tendency dominates contemporary music; certainly you can hear it in the alleged "lyrics" of pop songs, with their endless repetition, and their undisciplined lack of shape or design.

Perhaps the whole problem goes back to a misunderstanding of the nature of creativity. Of course the artist must be allowed spontaneity and room to express his feelings. Unfortunately that isn't enough to produce anything worthwhile. Everyone – artist or non-artist – has to learn his craft, and to study its disciplines.

Even the most naturally gifted painters, musicians, and writers painstakingly study their trades, usually all their lives, quite often for very skimpy rewards. The sloppy ones, the fakes and phonies, who rely on cheap effects and easy sensationalism, and whose real gift is often for self-promotion, may make a great deal of money very easily. They grab their allotted fifteen minutes, and then become famous for being famous. But they can't really achieve artistry, they are never truly creative, because they haven't learned the tools of their trade.

There are good arguments for changing English to a genuinely phonetic language. G. B. Shaw kept up an unremitting battle for this cause, and I can't improve on his arguments; they are logically unassailable. Unfortunately, English is not a logical language. I think it could be argued that Latin is logical, French is logical in some ways, but English is illogical almost to the point of lunacy.

In any case, language – especially spoken language – is intransigent. I've probably already leaned too hard on the linguistic equivalent of Gresham's Law, and the perverse tendency to choose the worse over the better in language, but it does illustrate the difficulties confronting anyone who attempts to reform (for example) spelling.

Having now persuaded myself that deliberate and conscious reform of language is impossible, I should stop writing this book. But I am no more logical than the language I speak, write, and love, and I decline to stop. Supposing, by wasting all this time, I nevertheless persuade *one person* not to say eck cetera, not to write alright for all right; I will not have lived in vain. If somewhere in the world, after reading this book, one person will stop saying "Lay down, Sir!" to his dog, and will instead suggest politely that it should lie down, I'll be happy and grateful.

There are a few rules of spelling which are sometimes helpful. For example, there is a group of words like *practice* (noun) and *practise* (verb) where you can be fairly safe by remembering that the noun is spelled with a *c* and the verb with an *s*. I mentioned the mnemonic earlier: *ice* is a noun, and *is* is a verb; unfortunately, ice is sometimes a verb, too, as in icing the puck or the cake. In the U.S., they are now spelling nouns and verbs alike with an *s* (e.g. defense), although they insist on making "practice" a verb; in England, they stick to the noun-c, verb-s pattern. In Canada, we typically sometimes do it one way, sometimes the other.

Another rule is the "I before E, except after C, and when pronounced AI, as in neighbour and weigh." But it is not very reliable, since it leaves out seize, weird, leisure, height, either, neither, foreign, forfeit, and only works on sheik, inveigle and heinous if they are correctly pronounced, which they rarely are.

During my teaching years, I once made a collection of words which almost none of my students knew how to spell. They were, in alphabetical order: all right (they spelled it alright, which is all wrong); accommodate, where the double consonants are a hazard; conscious and conscience, which invariably appeared without the second c; consensus, which has only one c, but which seems to ask for more; definitely, a word they loved but which took many strange forms; explanation, which became explaination; occasionally and occurrence – everyone wants to put an extra s in the former, and only one r in the latter; and suspense, which has s right through.

These are tricky words, which confuse even good natural spellers, but they can be learned if you put your mind to it.

CHAPTER

12

Trippingly on the Tongue: Casualties of Pronunciation

For years the top casualty of the anti-literacy campaign has been *nuclear*, increasingly rendered as *nucular*. Now come on, you guys. *Look at the word*. NUCLEAR. Where do you get that extra "u"? Since I don't have phonetic symbols on my printer (and since they're useless to anyone who would abuse a word in this way, in any case), let me give the closest possible approximation to the correct pronunciation. NEW-KLEE-AR. I haven't kept track of the offenders on this one; the list would be longer than Deuteronomy. Granted that English pronunciation is as mad as English spelling, mispronunciations are often excusable. *Nucular* is pure perversity.

Next exhibit is a related error: jubulant for jubilant. Several top CBC names are offenders – Liz Palmer, Jason Moscovitz and Hannah Gartner, in living memory. Are you listening, Liz, Jason, Hannah? The word is jubILant, not jubULant. Pronunciation exactly as it's spelled: there's absolutely no excuse for such howlers. In passing, please note that there is no *u* in escALator, meaning a moving stair. An esculent is something edible; don't touch it until you're quite sure you have good control on escalator. And only one *u* in *nuptials*: please, no *nuptuals*.

It was saddening to hear a theatre reviewer, discussing the Stratford production of *Timon of Athens*, accuse Timon of being a "misanthorp". In the course of a shortish review, he also was guilty of "wrecking vengeance" and turning profligate into proFLIGate. Where do they get these people? If you can't pronounce these not very difficult words, or at least look them up in a dictionary, what

63

right have you to review Shakespeare? How do you get the nerve to stand in front of a microphone on network radio and say "misanthorp"?

A friend has just contributed another howler: Hypmatize and its noun, hypmasis. She heard this continually, unapologetically repeated on a purportedly serious radio program. This was once a joke pronunciation by people who knew better but were indulging in mild facetiousness, or perhaps avoiding pomposity. It used to seem rather amusing but alas, it's dangerous: Classyists invariably pick up such jests and use them straight.

So please – HYPnotize and hypNOsis.

Here follows my little list of sounds that never will be missed. A strange new vogue has arisen for *afFLOOence* – low-literate for *affluence*, emphasis on first syllable, AFFluence. By contagion, we're also hearing *inFLOOence*. For years and years everyone pronounced influence properly, with the accent on the first syllable. But often recently I've heard it shifted to the second – only today a country and western singer Classyfied on the important inFLOOences in her work . . . oh Mr. Gresham, thou art mighty yet! If there's a choice, they'll inevitably choose wrong.

Burry: I thought this one had died – and been buried – long ago, but I heard it quite recently from CBC reporter Jane Antoniak. Pronounced to rhyme with *scurry*, it is Low-literate for *bury*, to inter, which is correctly pronounced as if it were spelled *berry*.

ConcoMITTant, someone said recently, possibly influenced by mittens, as it was cold day. The accent should be on the second syllable *conCOMitant*.

Dyper: A hopeless case, I know. Nevertheless, *diaper* has three syllables, not two. It should be pronounced DIE-AH-PR. It has not always meant napkins to cover a baby's behind (they were known as "nappies" when I was a girl), but had a variety of interesting applications. Look it up!

Essentric: Slovenly for *eccentric* which is pronounced EKcentric. Note also the recurrent *Assessory* for *accessory*, correctly pronounced AKsessory.

Heenious, haynious: This is intended for *heinous*, pronounced HAYNUS. Why not look up the pronunciation in a dictionary before making yourself ridiculous in public? And while we're at it *ridicklus* will not do. RID-IK-YOU-LUSS.

Inarresting: Slovenly for *interesting.* This is pure sloppiness, and many big names (e.g. Stuart MacLean, who teaches at a university as well as interviewing for CBC, and a faulty question beggar to boot) are guilty. Correct pronunciation: *intr*isting. Accent on first syllable. Slovenliness is also accountable for "Congradjulations," beloved of Peter Gzowski and thousands of others. Nevertheless, it's congraTulations. That's a *t*, not a *dj*.

A short time ago, yet another CBC luminary was suffering from laryngitis. She got that right, but where do you think this ailment was located? In her larnyx. If it were a larnyx, you'd have larnygitis. This cavity in the throat, with its cartilaginous walls containing the vocal cords, is the LARYNX. Plural, larynges, but we don't have to worry about them: we only have one. Larynges are for the birds only.

Mischeevious: Ugh. The host of CBC's Saturday afternoon Radio Show was responsible for this distortion of *mischievous.* It was commonly used by the uninstructed when I was young, but I thought everyone had been educated and ridiculed out of it long since, as I hadn't heard it for years. Accent on the first syllable, *MISS-chiv-us.*

Strenth: This is less common than it used to be, but in the Christmas holidays a record by Gordon Lightfoot, in which *strenth* was praised, was played repeatedly. Now, Gordon, why would you sin a son with a word like that in it? Can't you see that *strength* has a *g* in it (as does *length*, which often comes out *lenth*). You don't urge people to be *stron*, do you?

Pastoral, Plethora: Have I mentioned these somewhere else? Accent on first syllable, in both cases. Many otherwise reliable speakers (like Dale Goldhawk, of Cross Country Check-up) insist on accenting the second syllable.

Yuman Although in other respects, I love Carl Sagan this side of idolatry, he curdles my blood when he perverts human into yuman. H is not pronounced Y, huh?

We should also note the incidence of Classy in pronunciation, where people want to use a fancy word but don't take the trouble to learn how to pronounce it. In this class we have *takit* for *tacit*, correctly pronounced as if the *c* were an *s*, tassit. *Internecine* also has a sibilant *c*, as does *taciturn*, which should not be rendered as *takiturn.* Such words as *antipodes* and *terpsichore* are usually dragged into the conversation in the belief that such Classy stuff will really impress listeners. But they won't, if *antipodes* is made to rhyme with "toads", and *terpsichore* with "bore". Those final syllables are pronounced: AN-TIP-OH-DEES; TERP-SIK-OR-EE. On the same principle, hyperbole does not rhyme with roll; HIGH-PURR-BOWL-EE.

Related to Classy, but not quite identical, is something (glanced at earlier) that might be classified as Genteel, or Refained. This is most conspicuously exemplified by the Awk Squad, inventors of the colour Awqua, perversion of aqua, Latin for water, source of *aquatic* and various other English words; it's pronounced like the *a* in AMoeba, or florAL. You can't say awquatic, without spraining a tonsil, nor yet awmoeba, or florawl. A recent example of Awk-speak is the name of Robert Campeau, now unnecessarily refained as Cawmpeau. I wonder if these people amuse themselves by going cawmping?

CHAPTER

13

Mind the Stop:
Comma Sense

The purpose of punctuation is not to complicate a writer's or reader's life, but to be helpful in communicating meaning. You must ask yourself, as you hesitate over a punctuation mark, whether your meaning is clear to the reader as the sentence stands, or whether it's going to be a confusing jumble. If it doesn't make sense at first reading, the right punctuation may help.

My personal preference is for minimal punctuation. Never use a comma if your meaning is clear without it. However, this is not a rule – just my preference. As a student teacher, I once sat through a terrible "model" class in which a teacher forced students to memorize and recite the uses of the comma. I disagreed with most of them. One was that you must always use a comma after the conjunction "but". But why, I longed to ask, if the meaning is clear without it?

A current trend in punctuation which I find irritating is the abandonment of the dash. My keyboard has no dash, and I have had to use a hyphen with spaces on each side - like so. My poor editor has had to mark each of these with a proofreading symbol to indicate that it is a two-space dash, not a one-space hyphen. However, many publications are using hyphens for dashes in a way that is downright infuriating for the reader. How do you tell when they mean to join two words, as with a hyphen, or to separate them, as with a dash, when they use the same sign for both? Thus *Shape* magazine discusses "the deep posterior spinal muscles-which are not developed by typical back-extension exercises." In the same issue (August 1987) there is a description of a spa featuring early-morning walks, skin-care treatment, low-calorie meals, 45-minute gymnastics, and special baths for which "mud and water from the Dead Sea-famous since ancient times for their soothing, restorative qualities-are imported." (p.50) Secretarial courses are also teaching this silly and confusing style, for no reason that I can discover.

Three dots (. . .) indicate an omission, or ellipsis, in quoted material. They should not, in formal writing, be used for any other purpose. They are a temptation if one is too lazy to decide what the correct punctuation should be, or if one wants to suggest a sentence trailing off unfinished, in dialogue. The dots are much beloved of advertising copywriters; in fact, some of them use no other punctuation, apart from exclamation points. The three dots were brutally proscribed by the editor of a magazine on which I toiled in my youth; he said they were the trademark of the amateur. More specifically, the *female* amateur. Sometimes, when I wanted a little danger in my life, I would leave some copy on his desk with lots of . . . s, for the sport of hearing the yells of rage and disgust that filled the air when he read it.

Illegal dots (i.e., other than for indicating an omission) are a danger sign. Generally, when I find myself . . .-ing, I know it's time to quit for a while and take the dog for a walk.

A very common form of malpractice is the use of unnecessary quotation marks; another of the crimes to be laid at the door of the advertising fraternity. The following gem may not be word for word, as I didn't copy it down, but it gives you the idea:

> HI!!!! Come in to "Crazy" Jerry's BIG "WEEKEND" SALE . . . you've never seen such wild "Bargains"! Have we got a "Deal" for YOU! Your "credit" is good at "Crazy" Jerry's!

Crazy Jerry's quotation marks have no function at all, except to annoy punctuation buffs.

Quotation marks are also misused when the writer isn't quite sure of what he's talking about. Instead of checking a dictionary, he puts the unfamiliar word in quotes, as a sort of apology.

> Ed, he'd had a couple hits of like acid, y'know, and he seen this face, like sort of a like, "ephipany", y'know?

I made that one up. Just couldn't put my hand on an authentic example. But that's a good approximation. The spelling of epiphany is an artistic touch for authenticity.

Crazy Jerry's advertisement, above, exhibits a second punctuation vice which should be avoided. The exclamation mark should be used sparingly. If it is over-used, it loses all its emphatic quality: the more exclamations, the less impact. It's like someone yelling at the top of his lungs; after a while you tune him out completely. As for the multiple exclamation point – my feeling is that it has no place in civilized writing whatsoever. I once had an editor who believed that multiple exclamation points were intrinsically comic, and that every joke should be followed by a long string of them, presumably adding to the fun. She kept putting them into my copy, I kept erasing them. Took a lot out of both of us.

Just ran across another example of quotation-mark-madness in our local weekly:

> People are asking "what in the world" (usually the language is more "colourful") Scott was doing in China . . . in the first place. Scott claims he was there on a "human rights mission" . . . [if he is] truly interested in "human rights" during this time of "economic depression", he would "stay home" and do some thing concrete . . . They want to know why he was in China "playing his fiddle" while "Canada was burning".

The columnist clearly has no idea of the real function of the quotation mark, and his promiscuous use of it makes it meaningless.

I've been trying to find a good book on punctuation, which I might recommend to readers. The best one, so far, is the frequently mentioned *Questions You Always Wanted to Ask About English*. My personal system of punctuation was formed by reading; one of the strongest influences was *The New Yorker*.

There are certain questions of punctuation (notably one concerning quotation marks) on which I can never make up my mind, and two of the best editors I know belong to diametrically opposed schools on the matter. Sometimes both styles look wrong to me, and then I go by feelings rather than rules, and am inconsistent. I'm not recommending this system, I'm just being truthful.

Most books on punctuation are arbitrary and inflexible, hooked on rules, and I haven't found them very useful. When in doubt, ask someone you trust to read your material and note where communication fails for lack of punctuation. Re-reading is indispensable, for catching errors of all kinds.

CHAPTER

14

Foreign Classy

A subdivision of Classy pronunciation has produced some strange manifestations in the use of allegedly French expressions. Now a sound training in grammar is immeasurably strengthened by study of a second or third language, and in the dear dead days beyond recall, French and Latin were required for matriculation, so that all high school students had at least a smattering of them.

Useful for understanding grammar generally. Useless for understanding the language in question. French was abominably taught – exactly as if it were a dead language. We never heard spoken French, and the pronunciation was mangled into a ghastly gobbledegook that had no resemblance to any form of human speech.

When parents and students complained that no one was learning to speak French, the establishment replied that their mandate was to teach students to read and write grammatical French: afterwards, if someone wanted to speak French, they could do it, but high school was not the place for such frivolities. It is to this theory that we are indebted for the excruciating noises produced by Michael Wilson and John Crosbie and Don Blenkarn in the name of bilingualism. Should be forbidden by law. On pain of death.

It took years of work to undo the evil effects of this teaching, and when we went to university, or studied in France or Quebec, it was humiliating to have our mentors blench with horror, or burst into howls of merciless Gallic laughter.

"You studied at an Ontario high school? My poor child, you have learned the worst French in the world, in the whole history of the world." That was a charming old gent in Montreal, who laboured incessantly to correct my deplorable accent. I now speak reasonably good French, but only because I've worked like a dog at it ever since I got out of high school. Without regular practice, it gets rusty, whereas if one learns it properly from a very young age, one retains it much more securely.

However, the schools did teach French grammar, and students' understanding of language structure was strengthened. Learning spoken French was largely a matter of undoing the terrible damage done in high school, but it was useful to know the irregular verbs and the adjectives that precede the noun (although we had to memorize them in English: fineprettyuglygoodbadbiglargesmall-youngoldnew).

Latin was also a requirement for university entrance in those far-off days. Studying Latin gives one a really firm grounding in grammatical structure: realization that nouns and pronouns have cases, persons, and numbers, while verbs have moods, tenses and conjugations. I very nearly dropped Latin at one point; a course in book-keeping was being offered, and my best friend – who made all the decisions in our lives – advised that we must drop Latin and take bookkeeping. Then we would be able to get jobs and buy lots of clothes, a project for which Latin was no use at all.

Luckily, my Latin teacher talked me out of it. "You'll need Latin to get into university," he warned me. I explained that I wasn't going to university because we didn't have enough money, but he persisted, and talked to my parents, who were dubious about my future as a bookkeeper anyway. As a result, when I did get into university, I had the requirements. Sorry about this digression into my private life, but I think it's relevant, and I repeat: the development of a firm foundation for good English is a demanding business, and it should begin early, in public school, with a thorough grounding in grammar by a teacher who knows his/her stuff. I realize that Latin has all but disappeared, except in posh private schools, because it has little practical immediate value (in getting jobs, etc.). I realize that it's a lost cause, but would like merely to suggest that it may be in some ways, a pity, and that in the long-term view a few years of Latin might pay off.

French is being taught quite differently now, and there is a good chance that even people from ordinary schools (as distinguished from French Immersion or Posh American) can acquire a command of the language.

In the meantime, however, we have to deal with the unlovely phenomenon of French Classy for which, again, I hold the media largely responsible.

Exhibit A: *debockle*, a frightful rendering of the French *débacle*. This is pronounced, if one can express French pronunciation without phonetic symbols, roughly DAY-BAC(l), the *l* subvocalized. *Debockle* and *daybockle* are anglicizations, in the Michael Wilson manner. *Dubble awntend* is a bastardization of *double entendre*, French for double meaning. Why not just say double meaning instead of putting half of it in English, half in dubious French? If we're going to use French, it's something like *doobl abntahnd(r)*. Some French sounds really don't have an English equivalent. A similar bastardization occurs (far too frequently) in *paper mashay*, for *papier mâché*, literally, chewed-up paper. If we're going to have *mâché*, pronounced approximately as if it were French, why put the *paper* part in English? *Pap-yay mahsh-ay* is a rough approximation of the French pronunciation. *Coup de grace* – that *grace* is pronounced *grahs*, not *grah*, as in Stewart Maclean's Classy rendition, and the French don't pronounce the final *p* in *coup*, which sounds like coo, not coop.

Insooisance: This extraordinary word was produced by Sheila Shotton (15 September '90) on CBC's nice, lovely, wonderful, saccharine weekend programme, "Fresh Air," which is so sweet it induces diabetes. Sheila was trying for *insouciance* – describing someone very cool and nonchalant. Dat's a good woid, Sheila, but if we're going to be as Classy as all that, why not get the pronunciation right? It's French, after all: *ahn-soos-ee-abnce* is about as close a rendition as I can manage. Or anglicize it: *in-soos-ee-ance*. I must confess to a guilty weakness for *insouciance* myself; it expresses a nice don't-give-a-damn attitude. But we must learn to pronounce it, mustn't we, Sheila?

Saw-tay is Classy for *fry*. It purports to represent *sauter* (imperative *sautez*). French pronunciation, roughly *soh-tay*. It means to jump, skip, leap. I asked a French cook about it, and she said that it was used in the phrase *faire sauter une crêpe* – to flip a pancake. She also conceded that *pommes de terres sautées* was permissible, but our general use of *sauter* for *fry* simply didn't exist in French. What did they say? "Cuire," she said. Just plain cook. However, I've since encountered some disagreement on this, and a frying-pan is a *sauteuse*. I've also seen, in an advertisement for frying-pans, *sautière*, though none of my dictionaries acknowledge it. But please don't pronounce the first syllable as "saw."

Dearest to the heart of the Classy speaker is *Or Derv*, Michael Wilsonese for *hors d'oeuvre*, pronounced by the French roughly *or dhvr.* (By Don Blenkarn Hor Doov.) The *v* comes before the *r*, Michael. The *h* is silent, Don. In English, these little mouthfuls are called appetizers – quite as accurate, and infinitely easier for Anglophones to pronounce. The pronunciation of the plural is the same as the singular; the final s is silent, as is the initial h.

A *chaise longue*, while we're at it, is a comfortable place to lounge, but it doesn't mean a lounge chair; it's a long chair. The *chaise* part starts with a *sh* sound, not a *ch*.

Pott pourri: This highly inelegant pronunciation of *pot pourri* was Classy in intent; it was the specialty of Larry Zolf, on CBC's morning show. I believe it was intended to mean something like miscellaneous, a collection of odd bits. *Pot* in French is pronounced to rhyme with know, or as near as makes no matter; one should know better than to pronounce *pot* to rhyme with bought.

A *cachet of weapons:* This was the work of Sue Prestage, on the "Four to Six Show." I suspect she meant a *cache* (pronounced like cash) meaning something hidden. *Cachet*, pronounced cashay, is a distinguishing mark, evidence of authenticity, prestige . . . hardly applicable to the fruit of a drug bust.

A good rule of thumb, for avoiding such egregious errors: if you haven't studied the language, don't attempt to use it. It's not a disgrace to speak English. Why not say "appetizer" instead of mangling Or Derv? What's wrong with saying "and so forth" rather than perpetuating Eck Cetera? Even when they're used correctly, some foreign phrases are ridiculous: I recently read a conference report that gabbled about "avian piscivores." I'll bet the author thought it sounded Classy, and that people would think he was really clever! But it only means fish-eating birds, after all, and even with no more than high school Latin, I could figure it out, and I thought he was a jerk to drag in that pretentious phrase instead of saying it in English.

Sometimes there's a French word that perfectly expresses just what we want to say (*le mot juste*, in fact) when there isn't a precise equivalent in English. It's a temptation to use such phrases, but really, unless we're prepared to take the trouble to find out how to pronounce them properly, our little excursions into bilingualism produce shudders of agony among our French friends.

The French are intolerant of abuse of their language, wincing eloquently at errors in pronunciation and grammar. Interestingly, while they believe it's almost blasphemous to speak bad French, it's perfectly acceptable for them to speak horrible English; it may even be cute. The reasoning behind this curious double standard seems to be that French is a beautiful, precise, and elegant language; to use it inaccurately or sloppily is not only sacrilegious but a betrayal of ignorance and bad taste.

English, however, is an ugly, slovenly, and generally deplorable language, so that it really doesn't matter what you do to it, and anyone who criticizes your pronunciation of "Thursday" is practising racial discrimination. I once had a French professor who swore up and down that the English word for a dinner-jacket was a "Smoking"; when we suggested that this was a purely French usage, which never occurred in English, he jeered at our ignorance. There was once such a thing as a smoking-jacket, which gentlemen wore when they smoked, so that their ordinary clothes would not smell offensively of tobacco; my grandfather had several, but they disappeared with his generation. But my French professor would have none of it. I daresay he still wears his Smoking when he goes to dinner parties.

No doubt we often cause our French friends severe pain, but we also give them many belly laughs, as they do us with such absurdities as the Smoking.

A curious practice among certain Anglophones occurs through the conviction, when they encounter an unfamiliar word, that a simple phonetic pronunciation cannot be right. They don't look it up in a dictionary, of course, but arbitrarily assign it an exotic and improbable sound, possibly hoping that it will intimidate listeners into thinking it must be right. An acquaintance of mine, for example, always pronounces Proust as Prst, rejecting the obvious Proost as not French enough, perhaps. *Croissant* becomes croosant, and *chartreuse* sh'troosh.Another lady who fancies herself as a botanist pronounces anemone as anenema, and turns fungus into something like foonjioos.

French and Latin are of course not the only languages to suffer abuse. A lady broadcaster, describing a glittering event, announced that "all the *hoi polloi*" of Toronto's artistic and literary world were on hand. I daresay a few *hoi polloi* may cling to the skirts of the artistic and literary world, but it's unlikely they were at the party. They were probably clutching their wine bottles down in the ravine, or fumbling their way toward a Salvation Army hostel. The *haut monde* may have been at the party, ma'am, but wouldn't it be a good idea to make sure you know what you're talking about before broadcasting your ignorance on network radio? The *hoi polloi* are the masses, the rabble, the underprivileged, and the expression is usually intended slightingly.

Remember a phrase that I quoted earlier: "One criteria of excellence is performance." Yes, indeedy. But you can't have one criteria, because criteria is plural. The singular form is criterion. You can have one criterion, but if you get two of them, they have to be criteriA. Will the Hon. Barbara MacDougall please note? I heard her, in a "Morningside" interview, talking about "those criterias."

Foreign plurals give us all sorts of difficulties. Let's look at a few more from the same stable as "one criteria."

Phenomenon also comes from a Greek root, and forms its plural by changing the "on" to "a." One phenomenon, two phenomena. Please, spare us "this phenomena."

Basis, crisis, diagnosis, ellipsis form the plural by changing "is" to "es." One basis, two bases. One crisis, two crises. Imperfectly assimilated, this rule has led to a vague belief that "bases" and "crises" have more class than their singular form, and we constantly hear the screwed-up version: "On this bases . . ." If it's *this*, it's a *basis*. "Some kind of a state of crises," said a university professor in yet another "Morningside" interview. Notice that *a? A state.* That means there's only one, so it must be "a state of crisis." You don't say crises or bases unless you have more than one. Of each.

Stratum, datum, medium. These Latin words form their plural by changing the *um* to *a.* (But all Latin words don't form plurals this way, so don't start any Classy analogies.) You can't therefore have *a media.* "This media" was a favourite phrase among media instructors at a certain Community College.

Vortex, index. The plurals are *vortices, indices.* If you want to say vortexes and indexes, no one should object – it's a legitimate anglicization. However, Vickie Gabereau got her tongue tangled on this one, though (as mentioned) one has to be tolerant of such matters on a live show. Her guest was talking about the mysterious circles which periodically appear in grain fields, and which the lunatic fringe naturally attributes to space aliens. He suggested that the cause was meteorological – vortices of air; Vickie responded with a query about "this vortices". I was prepared to be generous about this (most of the time she's pretty reliable) but later I caught her insisting that she could care less. Twice in one programme.

A few miscellaneous foreign language nuisances, some of them so deeply entrenched that I have no hope of change. Consider the now universal (with one exception) misuse of the word circumstances. *Circum* means around, about. The circumference of a circle is the encompassing boundary or periphery (but not its parameter!). That is, circumstances are around you, not above you. So why does everyone in the world say "Under the circumstances?" Because they never think of what words mean, that's why.

Per se. Basically, per se is, like, stuck into sentences simply as padding, like like, basically, etc. It was considered really Classy at one time, but is now simply an unnecessary noise, used without any reference to its meaning. Correctly used, it means "by or in itself, intrinsically", terms which occur rather infrequently in ordinary speech. I have never been able to decide what the Classyists intend by their use of it; possibly they haven't either. They just think it sounds kinda classy.

15

Mad Metaphors

A dubious practice among teachers of English is that of forcing children to decorate their writing with figures of speech. They are required to write stories and essays which incorporate a number of metaphors and similes – an agonizing exercise, which produces some of the worst writing, with the least spontaneous images in the history of language. It should be forbidden by law, with severe penalties.

This sadistic activity arises from a misunderstanding of the creative process. It isn't developed by practice. Images should flash upon one, in a kind of revelation; and they will, too, if you become a good observer of the world about you, and if you read work in which metaphor is used successfully, so that you see how it's done.

I don't believe, for example, that T. S. Eliot slogged away practising similes, so that when he looked at a twilight sky one day, he was perversely reminded, not of a beautiful sunset, but of "a patient etherized upon a table". Raymond Chandler is an excellent exponent of vigorous imagery. At one point, his detective, Marlowe, finding himself in flossy and pretentious surroundings, feels as welcome "as a louse on a wedding cake". Carnally watching a pretty girl, he lost interest when ". . . she opened a mouth like a fire bucket and laughed . . . the hole in her face when she unzipped her teeth was all I needed". Another of his unforgettable images was his description of a blonde (Chandler and Marlowe loved/hated blondes obsessively): ". . . a blonde. A blonde to make a bishop kick a hole in a stained-glass window." Now that's a blonde, and that's an image you remember. I can't remember which book it comes from, and someone has borrowed/stolen all my Chandler, so I can't check. But the line and the beautiful image of the kicking bishop has stayed ineradicably in my mind.

You can't teach that kind of thing by practice exercises. All you can do is encourage your students to read good metaphor-makers, and learn to look at the world. If you try to teach it by rule and rote, you fall into the Miss Groby trap. Remember James Thurber's Miss Groby, prototype of the teacher who tries to reduce English to a formula, and who produces generations of literature-haters? I would quote you an illustrative passage, but all my Thurber has disappeared: poltergeists? Never mind. Everyone should read "Here Lies Miss Groby" for themselves. In passing, a warning: never lend books, and always search your guests' luggage before you let them out of the house.

Peter de Vries had a lot of fun mocking literary devices. Attending, against his will, a jolly sleigh-ride, he moodily watches the moon rise – first like a rotten orange, then like a bloody cliché.

These are the professionals. Most of the time, unfortunately, the use of metaphor detracts from the desired effect, rather than adding to it. For instance, CBC interviewer Christopher Thomas described a place as being "steeped in ghosts". Now come on, Christopher. *To steep* means to soak in water. So that just won't wash, huh?

A great favourite, currently, is "to coin an old phrase" and its alternate, "to coin the old cliché". This arises from a misunderstanding of the meaning of both *coin* and *cliché*, which do NOT mean to use, or to repeat. To coin is to manufacture money by stamping metal. If you coin something, it must by definition be new – you've just stamped it out, this minute. You can't coin an old coin, an old phrase, an old anything. Metaphorically, to coin is "to invent or fabricate (esp. new word or phrase)". You cannot, I repeat, invent or fabricate something that's already old.

Stipulation: the phrase can be used ironically, with a deprecating smile. You catch yourself using some weary old cliché – "he's as strong as an ox" – and so you add, facetiously, "to coin a phrase". Classy speakers should not attempt mild jests of this type, for they are sure to screw them up.

Again, it is impossible to coin a cliché. Wrong metaphor. You have to know what words mean to use metaphors successfully. A cliché was originally a metal casting of stereotype or electrotype. Once cast, there was no changing it. Thus it takes on the metaphorical meaning of something locked in, unchangeable, unoriginal, hackneyed. *Not coined.*

Carol Verdun, of *The Independent*, provided me with a nice instance of metaphor-madness, from an Atlanta newspaper:

> "I hope I can help Dan," Campbell said. "I'm going to work my tail off for him. We've got to get in the pits now, put our nose to the jugular vein and go after it."

Campbell's gift is for mixing metaphors. "Going for the jugular vein" usually means attacking with lethal intent: with a knife, if the agent is human, with teeth if it's an animal, or possibly a vampire. The nose is usually applied to the grindstone, implying not slaughter but dedication and hard work.

Another category badly in need of correction is what might be labelled "phoney imagery". That is, it pretends to be a simile or metaphor, but is really just padding. Consider this by Leonard Cohen:

> Like a bird on a wire
> Like a drunk in a midnight choir
> I have tried, in my way, to be free.

What has a bird on a wire in common with a drunk in a choir, and why are they made parallel? Is this bird sitting on a telephone wire, like a starling, or a swallow preparatory to migration? Because they *are* free, and have no need to "try". In what other circumstances do birds sit on wires? Perches in cages are not made of wire. It doesn't make sense.

Now – about that drunk. What is he doing in a midnight choir, if he's drunk? Was he dragged there against his will? If he's there voluntarily, he's free, and doesn't have to try for something he already has achieved. Why would anyone drag a drunk into a choir, if he doesn't want to be there? Drunks are not desirable additions to choirs and most choir-leaders would prefer that they stay away.

In short, these phrases mean exactly nothing, and one is forced to the embarrassing realization that Mr. Cohen stuck them in to get a rhyme, because he was too lazy to work on a valid image. He was once a promising young poet, but he sold out long ago to the songwriting biz, since when he's written some ineffably bad stuff, though I dare say he's made a lot more money than he would have in the poetry biz, which is notoriously ill-paid.

That first verse is the best – correction: the least rotten – in the song. Later, Mr. Cohen rhymes *free* with *thee*. "I will try to make it up to thee." How could anyone with even vestigial rags of artistic conscience perpetrate a rhyme like that? And it doesn't scan – he has to squeeze the words into the beat. Nor is this poetic offence compensated by lovely sound: in another song, Mr. Cohen refers to his "golden voice", which in reality resembles the creaking on its rusty hinges of a badly corroded farm gate. In spite of which, CBC tirelessly inflicts these atrocities upon us, and pretends they're Art, although if an unknown person tried to sell songs as feeble as Cohen's, he would be laughed out of the business. Another example of the Canadian infatuation with Big Names as a substitute for art.

I digress; perhaps this belongs in the chapter on popular songs (Words and Music). But Mr. Cohen's recent *oeuvre* is bad in so many ways that one simply doesn't know where to put him.

Back to metaphors, then. My finest example of metaphor-madness occurred in a review in the Hamilton *Spectator* of a stage production of "Murder on the Nile". The criticism was extremely negative, although the review itself – as will be seen – could be used as an object lesson in bad writing. It nevertheless carried an unmistakeable aura of self-congratulation. Really Classy!

"The play struggles to maintain credulity in the face of some virtuoso subterfuge." Surely the struggle was to maintain *credibility*: why would anyone want to maintain *gullibility, readiness to believe on weak or insufficient grounds?* Our critic's problem is that he doesn't know what credulity means. What in the world "virtuoso subterfuge" may be I simply can't imagine. (I know what the words mean, taken separately, but together they make no sense: *special knowledge or skill in technique* of *evading censorship by deception*. Huh? Sound and fury, signifying nothing. As Polonius would have said, "It is an ill phrase, a vile phrase."

"Not even Dame Agatha can sustain the warren of convolutions that threaten to sink this feeble effort."

I'll bet Dame Agatha wouldn't mix her metaphors like that. Rabbits live in warrens, but convolutions don't. (They're twists, coils, or sensuous folds.) And how can you sustain this dubious warren, especially if it's (presumably) on a ship, since it's threatened with sinking? Warrens are underground rabbit towns.

"The action chugs at a yawning pace that is positively lethal." Yawning may be a sign of boredom but it is rarely lethal. I submit that "chugs" is an unsuitable word – if something is chugging along, it's usually making steady progress. It's when it drags that one feels like yawning. An inexcusably bad sentence.

"There are some unconscionably bad performances that verge on the edge of hysteria." If they're verging, they're already on the edge. "Canon Pennefather's throat was constricting with indignation." It may have been constrict*ed* with indignation, but it couldn't be constrict*ing* unless it had wound itself around something and was choking it – a good trick, for an old gentleman's throat.

"Stephen Russell is so garbled as to be unintelligible." His speech may have been garbled, but Mr. Russell himself could not easily have been, or his state would have been far worse than unintelligible. "Garble: To mutilate with a view to misrepresentation."

Finally,"Genevieve Caslin is amusing as a hustling lackey . . ." A lackey is by definition a man-servant. What on earth was Miss Caslin up to?

Sad stuff. It's odd that a man who writes as badly as this has the gall to criticize another's work. I didn't see the play, but it's difficult to believe that it could be as bad as the review. No doubt he believed his efforts at metaphor made it vivid, or even Classy. But metaphors don't work unless you think of their meaning, so that the review becomes a kind of exemplar of How Not To Use a Metaphor. It's the work of someone who really never thinks about the meaning of the words he uses, who doesn't seem even to realize that words do have definite meanings. If he ever thought about what a warren was, he couldn't have written that silly stuff about it sinking. He's just picked up words promiscuously, and stuck them in without thinking of making sense. How can anyone who writes as incompetently as this hold a job on a newspaper – or get one in the first place?

A note in passing on "promiscuously". I found that my use of the word sent some of my auditors into fits of laughter, an unexpected response. The hilarity derived, I discovered, from the fact that the word is frequently used in the phrase "sexual promiscuity." They believed this was its exclusive meaning. Sorry to disappoint you, guys, but there are other varieties of promiscuity. Promiscuous means "making no distinctions; undiscriminating; carelessly irregular; casual."

See how it works? If you look up a word in the dictionary, you have a lot more flexibility in its use. You can talk about promiscuity without being stuck with loose morals.

If you would like an example of a really effective metaphor at work, see Dylan Thomas's "Fern Hill". The whole poem is structured around the image of time, along with brilliant metaphorical use of colours.

Before I conclude this chapter, an apology to all guests whom I may have slandered, above. The Chandler image (blonde, bishop kicking hole in stained-glass window) is from *Farewell, My Lovely*, p. 78. Thurber is still missing.

CHAPTER

16

Politically Correct?

The Bare Naked Ladies, a Canadian pop group, was banned from performing at the City Hall's New Year's Eve celebration in Toronto, on the grounds that their name objectifies women. According to the musicians, who are male and fully clad, the name was chosen to evoke the period of innocence, perhaps around the age of eight or nine, when such terminology was a natural form of expression. Just why they wanted to evoke that period remains unclear. I suspect their real motive was to find an attention-getter: legitimate enough in their field. Their music (to my ears) is undistinguished but inoffensive. Their name doesn't make me feel like an object. The names of pop and rock groups defy logical analysis.

Nevertheless, the banning of Bare Naked Ladies has caused a great kefuffle: it is an exercise in political correctness, one of the more recent clouds on the horizon of language.

Political correctness is not the preserve of any particular group, and espouses no specific political or philosophical doctrine. President Bush has tried to blame it on "campus radicals"; John Taylor, in a *New York* magazine article, has inveighed against left-wing student extremists propagating the "new fundamentalism". These accusations were neatly refuted by Rosa Ehrenreich, in "What Campus Radicals?" (*Harper's*, December 1991). She claims that left-wing movements on campus are so small as to be nearly invisible, and that they have no voice. She once endeavoured to protest the Gulf War at an allegedly non-partisan rally of the Republican Club at Harvard; the organizers turned off the microphone when she tried to speak. Her unamplified voice was drowned out by a chorus of right-wing shouts.

Time characterizes the politically correct protesters as "cry-babies". They are not a movement, or a school of thought, but a heterogeneous group of hypersensitive protesters, who interpret anything and everything as an insult or an attack. Their motley quality was illustrated by picketers of the classic film "Fantasia". A group called Dieters United objected to the hippo ballerinas as ridiculing fat people. Religious fundamentalists were horrified at the acceptance of evolution in the Rite of Spring sequence. Even the Nut-cracker Suite passage aroused suspicion: those dancing mushrooms might be subtle propaganda for drug-addiction.

Political correctness is not pure lunacy, however. It has its roots in very real fears. Racial discrimination and anti-feminism are constant threats to the safety of minorities and women. Derogatory terms and vicious jokes can be very hurtful; there's no question but that we must learn to watch our language.

At the same time, we don't have to lose our sense of humour completely, and we don't have to cut off our noses to spite our faces.

A glaring example of this is the campaign to ban "incorrect" books from schools and libraries. One offender is *Huckleberry Finn*, condemned chiefly because of its casual use of the word nigger. But *Huck* is an invaluable means of teaching how racism works and thrives. Huck, though he is fundamentally good and decent, comes from the dregs of poor-white society; he nevertheless assumes axiomatically that he is superior because Jim is a nigger. He uses the abusive term without rancor or abusive intent, but it conveys the tacit contempt of the whites for the blacks. But slowly, imperceptibly, an awareness of Jim's great-heartedness and generosity overcomes Huck's ingrained prejudice. In a tremendous near-religious revelation, he realizes that he can't send Jim back to Miss Watson, although this is a betrayal of the conventional wisdom and morality which has shaped his thinking. "All right then, I'll *go* to hell," says Huck, and determines to get to work and steal Jim out of slavery. His thinking is muddled and incoherent; he doesn't have the words to express his recognition of the evil of slavery, but his whole world view has changed.

After this tremendous scene, the arrival of Tom Sawyer is a painful anti-climax. Tom eagerly joins Huck in rescuing Jim, but he knows that Jim has already been set free, and doesn't tell either Huck or Jim. He prolongs the imprisonment for sport, without a thought for Jim's feelings. He doesn't, as Huck has done, see him as his fellow-man; Jim is still a commodity, an object, to be used as a source of amusement.

The last chapter is almost unbearable, but if we throw out the book because of it, we also lose the splendid and subtle process by which Huck unconsciously grows out of racism, culminating in the wonderful moment of transcendence.

A friend has drawn my attention to an adaptation of *The Secret Garden* in which all mention of British colonial attitudes had to be deleted. The colonial attitude was a repugnant one, in all its manifestations; but what's the point of trying to pretend it didn't exist? What do we do about books like *Passage to India*, in which the colonial attitude is the key issue of the plot? It is surely one of the most powerful indictments of colonialism ever written: do we have to pitch it out, or censor undesirable bits? My friend tells me Kipling has been banned from most college and high school reading lists, so practically no one under forty has read him. Again, his "white man's burden" convictions are pretty hard to tolerate, but they were very much part of his period. How can we ever understand that period, and liberate ourselves from its errors, if we pretend it never existed? To read his books doesn't mean we endorse his philosophy. Further, there is a great deal more to Kipling than his rather awful patriotism. Must we defraud ourselves of the good stuff for fear the bad will infect our minds? *The Just-So Stories* were pure magic in my childhood. (When I read them to my son, we both found them too cutesy, and I had to cut out all the O, Best Beloveds.) In my teens I was a Kipling addict; later I thought he was the King of Corn. Now he seems to me a gifted but uneven writer, sometimes dreadful, sometimes brilliant; sociologically, he is extremely valuable for understanding the period.

Recently a controversy raged in Israel because Daniel Barenboim wanted to include some Wagner in a concert by the Israel Philharmonic. Wagner, of course, was a shocking anti-Semite, adopted as a musical patron saint by the Nazis. But surely music is apolitical? I can get along nicely without "Parsifal", but I would be very unhappy if I were permanently deprived of "Die Meistersinger". This kind of racial touchiness cries out for examination of motives.

They are impoverishing their children by using these standards for judging the arts. Shakespeare's *Othello* is endangered, because the black hero (one of the Bard's noblest) is called "an old black ram". *The Merchant of Venice* has been the subject of controversy for years because of alleged anti-Semitism; and yet Shylock's poignant "Hath not a Jew eyes?" speech is the most powerful plea in the English language against racial prejudice and intolerance.

There is a good deal of anti-Semitism in T. S. Eliot, in G. K. Chesterton, and even in Chaucer. Condescension to other nationalities, "the lesser breeds without the law", permeates English literature. We can't throw it all out. We have to be aware of it and know how to deal with it.

The word "nigger" is so loaded that few of us can bring ourselves to pronounce it. Nevertheless a faculty colleague of mine frequently referred to himself, facetiously, as "dis nigger". We argued for hours about what is now known as political correctness (though the term had not been coined at the time) and one such session ended with his saying, "We sure thrashed that one out, eh, Honky Gal?" to which I replied, "Yassuh, Rastus." He also called me Miz White Trash, Li'l Eva, and other names, while I addressed him as Uncle Tom, Lije, and so on.

At that time my household included a black cat, a black Labrador, and a black horse; no whim or design was involved in this preponderance of blackness. It just happened.

My politically incorrect friend was once at our place when the black menagerie had assembled in the garden, and was much diverted. He nicknamed them, in ascending order of size, Liggie Niggie, Big Nig, and the Bigger Nigger. The word had no fears for him; after all, he pointed out, it just means black. Same root as Niger, as in the river. For a long time I couldn't bring myself to say it, but the nicknames charmed me so much I overcame the block, only to be sternly rebuked by another person for using racist language. Useless to point out that the source of the names was himself black.

Let me make myself clear: I'm not arguing in favour of abuse names like nigger and kike and dago and so on, nor do I advocate colonialism or slavery. But it is ridiculous to pretend that they never existed, that we can make them go away by censoring all mention of them. To admit their existence is not to legitimate or approve them. Drag them out into the light and let's inspect them.

If the emancipated can have some fun with it, all the better: see "Blazing Saddles", where the black sheriff-hero (Cleavon Little) confuses a racist crowd by clutching himself by the neck, holding his own gun to his head, and shouting, "One false move and the nigger gets it!"

In any case, the harder we try to suppress these matters, the more persistently they reappear. The political correctness action has given Bare Naked Ladies the kind of publicity they could never have hoped for if they called themselves something non-objectifying like The Scarborough Singers.

17

Jargon, Gobbledegook, and Bafflegab

Every trade and profession produces its own language, often intimidating to the outsider; we are inclined to condemn them for deliberate obscurantism when in fact they may be entirely functional, and necessary.

New language has to be invented for new things. Computerspeak is a good example: it's an insider language, but it's necessary, since there was no terminology to cover its innovations. Instead of criticizing it as incomprehensible, we simply have to learn it. If we don't need to learn it, we can ignore it and leave it to the experts. I don't really care "to interface" someone for lunch, but it's less unappetizing than "doing" lunch. I suppose some spill-over is inevitable. War talk, for example, spills into totally unrelated areas: no one fails in any field nowadays. They bomb out, or crash.

I've been using a computer instead of a typewriter for four years now, but I can't speak the language at all. I don't need it, and I can't be bothered unless it's going to be useful. The only kind of mouse I recognize is the four-legged variety, and I can't tell a bit from a byte. My nine-year-old nephew speaks the language fluently, and is astonished, first, at my ignorance, and second, at the speed with which I can whomp out pages on my machine. I'm fast because I learned to type at the age of twelve; as far as I'm concerned, the machine is simply a more efficient typewriter. People keep telling me I'm not exploiting its potential, but I can't be bothered. If I need to know some more, I'll learn it; right now I have other priorities.

My nephew also knows the inside terminology of hockey,

whereas I (although I played shinny in my youth) wouldn't know how to ice the puck if my life depended on it. I've been driving a car for nigh on forty years, but my ignorance of what goes on under the hood causes my garageman real pain. But no more pain than he causes me, when (after long years in the trade), he hasn't learned to spell exeleratur (joke: should be accelerator, though there are several accepted variants). "So what?" we snarl at each other, when rebuked for inexcusable ignorance.

However, that kind of ignorance is okay. He knows what a carburetor is, even if he can't spell it, and that's what's important. He isn't setting up as a spelling expert. Like accelerator, carburetor has a wide variety of acceptable spellings (-ettor, etter); the man never hits on any of them. I suspect that those acceptable spelling variants entered the language through a sort of despair on the part of dictionary-makers: they gave up on trying to get people to spell the word correctly, and decided to accept the wrong spellings out of sheer fatigue. The same syndrome can be seen at work when they decide to concede the acceptability of (for example) nauseous, to mean nauseated, when in fact it means the opposite: a nauseous object is nauseating.

We shouldn't object to specialized or technical language; it develops out of necessity. Scientific papers are intimidating to most lay people, because we haven't acquired the necessary vocabulary to make sense out of them. If it's necessary for us to read this difficult stuff, we must either find an interpreter to help us, or must go to work and painfully learn the language. It can be done, though it's daunting.

However, we have a right to protest and object furiously to the infection of Classyspeak in any and all fields. I don't mind labouring through a tough paper on water-borne toxins, but it's annoying to be confronted with gobbledegook like avian piscivores, complained of earlier. Cultivate simplicity, I cry, with Charles Lamb. Let us have fish-eating birds, and down with avian piscivores and the like.

Doctors often have difficulty communicating with patients in comprehensible language, often leaving them more terrified of the strange words than of their actual illness. A teenager who consulted one of these non-communicators (for something like the 'flu) was panic-stricken by references to "dermal lesions" and "pustules". He thought he had some vile and mysterious disease, like AIDS or syphilis, whereas the doctor was trying to talk to him about pimples, and their possible source in poor dietary habits.

Other doctors lean over backwards to be colloquial, frequently irritating their clients with genial inquiries such as, "How are the waterworks?"

"I have no problems with elimination of urine, if that's what you mean," coldly replied one irritable patient.

It's hard to identify Classyspeak in academic writing, because many academics have lost the capacity for speaking or writing with simplicity and clarity. Here's Erich Auerbach, in an essay entitled *Fortunata:*

> An ethically oriented historiography, which also on the whole proceeds in strict chronological order, is bound to use an unchangeable system of categories and hence cannot produce synthetic-dynamic concepts of the kind we are accustomed to employ today. Concepts like "industrial capitalism" or "absenteeism," which are syntheses of characteristic data, applicable especially to specific epochs, and, on the other hand, concepts like Renaissance, Enlightenment, Romanticism, which first of all designate epochs but are also syntheses of characteristic data, sometimes applicable to epochs other than those originally designated by them, are designed to cover phenomena in motion; such phenomena are traced from their first sporadic appearance, then as they occur with progressive density, and finally as they abate and change and vanish; and an essential aspect of all these concepts if the fact that their growth and transformation – that is, an idea of evolution – is contained in them, is conceived as part of their content. On the contrary . . . (p. 19)

I'll spare you the contrary. It goes on and on. After reading it over several times, I believe he's suggesting that different historical periods produce their own languages, which evolve and become more complex with time. Well, that's not particularly startling or original – it's observable even by non-academics, and can be easily stated in simple words. Perhaps he's saying something much more profound, and I haven't been able to untangle it from the verbiage. Perhaps I'm stupid, but it doesn't say much for his style if one has to read and re-read, to figure out what he's talking about. The man is suffering from an academic disease which might be called "abstractionitis"; his vocabulary has no concrete terms. These abstractions have no real-life denotation for the reader to sink his teeth into. Life is too short to waste on the progressive density of ethically oriented historiography. For me, anyway.

I can't resist giving you another sample of literary criticism just to show you what English students are up against when they hit graduate school.

This little gem is from William Empson's *Seven Types of Ambiguity:*

> When a contradiction is stated with an air of conviction it may be meant to be resolved in either of two ways, corresponding to thought and feeling, corresponding to knowing and not knowing one's way about the matter in hand. Grammatical machinery may be assumed which would make the contradiction into two statements; thus 'p and -p' may mean: 'If a=a , then p; if a=a , then -p.' If a and a are very different from one another, so that the two statements are fitted together with ingenuity, then I should put the statement into an earlier type; if a and a are very like one another, so that the contradiction expresses both the need for and the difficulty of separating them, then I should regard them as an ambiguity of the seventh type corresponding to thought and knowing one's way about the matter in hand. (p. 196)

Profound, eh? I had to read the whole book once, over two hundred pages of it, and it was all like that. It was supposed to help me to understand Shakespeare and Milton and Donne, whom I read easily, with enjoyment, although Empson came close to spoiling them for me. I had an argument with my professor about the value of reading Empson – or wasting my time, as I tactlessly expressed it – and was given a severe lecture. No one who hadn't read Empson could possibly consider herself an educated person, said my prof; he was acknowledged to be one of the greatest of critics, and the admission that I found reading him a waste of time perhaps suggested that I was in the wrong field. I protested furiously that I loved Shakespeare and Milton and Donne, and so on, but Empson was a big fat useless bore. My prof. seemed to think that the only real value of Shakespeare & Co. was their provision of raw material for Empson to gnaw and worry.

Perhaps I was in the wrong field. I still think that struggling through *The Seven Types of Ambiguity* was one of the worst time-wastes of all my years in university. I'll bet Shakespeare wouldn't have wasted five minutes on it.

Can you stand one more? Here is Irene Kock of the Nuclear Awareness Project, writing in *Dialogue*, Spring, 1991, about disposal of radioactive nuclear waste by burial in the Canadian Shield:

> Movement from the generic concept to a specific site will demand demonstration of the capability of the proponent to make the necessary site selection on the basis of technical grounds and to undertake non-destructive testing of the rock mass to ensure that it meets acceptance criteria. How this will be demonstrated should be outlined in the environment impact statement.

On the same subject, Douglas Letterman, identifying himself as "a private citizen in Toronto" says, "The only safe way to dispose of nuclear wastes is to stop manufacturing them."

Thank God for Mr. Letterman.

A special form of literary jargon might be labelled the False Falcon gambit. A poet of my acquaintance was obsessed with falcons, and since he frequently wrote his poems all over the ceilings and walls of the place he lived (a sort of commune in which I was also temporarily staying) the rest of us had abundant opportunity to study them. It was impossible to escape them. I thought his falcons behaved oddly, for falcons, and I once asked him to explain a line in one of the poems. He told me that if I couldn't understand it, I must be sadly obtuse, and that poetry shouldn't have to be explained. "It should be sensually experienced."

There should be *no* analysis of poetry, you should just let it wash over you, so to speak; I longed to turn him on to Empson and the professor who believed that literary criticism was more important than the actual literature, and have them fight it out.

Further discussion revealed that, although our poet knew the falcon was a bird, and that it soared and swooped, this was the limit of his information. He didn't know it belonged to the hawk family, and at first refused to believe it was a carnivore. I told him I had once seen a sparrow-hawk, or merlin, catch and eat a sparrow; he was quite shocked, and suspected me of making it up. Falcons, he seemed to believe, were ethereal creatures which weren't concerned with crass material activities like eating.

"Can't you understand that I'm using it as a symbol?" he demanded contemptuously, and when I asked what it was a symbol of, he got so annoyed that I didn't dast push the matter further; he didn't actually threaten to hit me, but I had a distinct impression that further falcon-analysis might get me a fat lip.

I longed to ask why he wrote about birds without knowing anything about them, but didn't have the courage. Falcons have been sanctioned for poetic use by Gerard Manly Hopkins: an In image. Further, this poet believed you didn't have to know what you were talking about, when you wrote poetry. This is a serious disease from which many poets, or would-be poets, suffer, but a full discussion of it must await another occasion.

Advertising jargon has probably done more to debase language than any other area of endeavour. It doesn't have an abstruse terminology of its own, like sciences or computers. Its creators try to write vividly and evocatively, but they don't know any grammar or syntax. They also seem to lack any kind of ethical conscience.

"Cars that can do what they look like they can do." A few years ago, that was dinned in our ears by an incessantly-repeated commercial and I used to curse horribly, and swear great oaths never to buy a product manufactured by the fiends responsible for it. Unfortunately, I can't remember now which auto-maker was the guilty one. However, I'm not going to buy another car until they build a non-polluting one, and so I'm boycotting the lot.

Another rage-inducer also dates back several years, when I was constantly irritated by a commercial for some variety of confection which was "lavished with whipped cream, nestled with strawberries". One doesn't *lavish with*. Whipped cream may be lavished upon some thing, but it has to be in the active voice. Millionaires lavish jewels on their wives, or more probably their mistresses, but that doesn't mean you can say the ladies were "lavished with" jewels. Same with "nestle". Little birds (nestlings) may nestle in their nests; children may nestle, or cuddle down, in their beds, as they did in "The Night Before Christmas". But you can't nestle a cake with strawberries. If you want to get into the *Reader's Digest* for picturesque speech, you might say that the berries are nestling in the whipped cream. You can say that the cake is topped with strawberries and whipped cream, if you like. The more you try to get cutesy and colourful, the worse your commercial is likely to be.

These, of course, are only a few minor instances of the evils perpetrated by advertising, but it's not a subject I like to dwell upon, as it's bad for my blood pressure. I think it's interesting, though, that the purpose behind all this is to make us want to buy the product. Far too often, the effect is the exact opposite – it makes us loathe and detest the product, and swear never to buy it or anything else produced by its manufacturer. I used to enjoy an occasional beer, but beer commercials have almost made a teetotaller of me.

The world of sport has had some weird effects on language. Sports writers and broadcasters often suffer from suppressed feelings of inferiority; they think the rest of the journalistic world despises them as jocks and meatheads. In self-defence, some of them expend a lot of hard work on sounding Classy. Thus, Dave Perkins in the Toronto *Star*,

> In undoubtedly the singular greatest introduction one human being has ever given another, King presented World Boxing Council president Jose Sulaiman, some guy he has in one of his pockets, to the fight press in a 15-minute monologue . . . (March 16/91, p. B4)

Does he mean "the single greatest" or the "most singular"? Not the same thing, Dave.

Starsports' Garth Woolsey illustrates metaphor madness in an essay which describes the Leafs as being "on the highway to nowhere" and goes on to mix up his metaphors so unselectively that one suspects he can't think straight:

> . . . the Leafs appeared relatively flush in the glow of the dawning of the first season of the post-Ballard era. As the season progressed it was clear they were flush all right, but in a toilet-like swirl . . . Ballard often was seen as a perverse meddler, the franchise's rot at the top. His successors have improved the window-dressing, brought old Leafs back into the fold . . . But it does seem an opportunity squandered. At every turn, the Leafs say they're charting a new course, but wind up lost at another, or the same old, dead end . . . The situation this season cried out for change, but that change could as easily have been a new era of stability as continued manic shuffling of the same old tattered deck. (March 16/91, 74)

Harold Ballard has left us, and I miss him daily. He could always be relied on to do something rich and strange to the language; I particularly recall one interview with Barbara Frum, whose questions he resented. He told her he was fed up with media types taking shots at him. "I don't know why I should be succoombed to this kind of crap," said Harold. We shall not see his like again.

I've been strongly urged to watch Don Cherry, who – according to some language theorists – is Harold's spiritual heir. Dedicated though I am to the cause, I just can't. However, I do watch the news and here one can't escape the Cherry family. Mrs. Cherry has made a commercial in which she tells us of the various headicks in her life. "When I get headicks, I get them!" When she has a pain in her pinny, does she complain of stomachicks?

Ache is onomatopoeic. That long, agonized *a* suggests pain and suffering, which is lost completely if you degrade it to an *ick*. Couldn't someone have given Mrs. C. a little coaching? How can anyone look at *ache* and pronounce it *ick*?

Military Classy is a special subdivision, not to be confused with dangerous practices such as disinformation and propaganda. (See Chapter 22.) Its intention seems to be much the same as all Classy use: to sound important and knowledgeable. In the Military specialization, the method is to tack on extra prefixes and suffixes; in a CBC interview, a military authority regaled us with *encaution*, *deploymentation*, *remediate*, and *coronate*. The latter, I think, was Classy for the old-fashioned verb *to crown*, the thing that happens at a coronation. Other favourites in Military Classy use are *analyzations*, *resonations*, and *rigidizations*. I've noticed *remediate* creeping into general use, presumably because the verb to remedy isn't sufficiently Classy. *Analyzation* is taking over from plain old analysis. It's interesting that among the military, nobody ever dies; they merely suffer mortal consequences. (Bombing-out and crashing, slang for dying, are not Military.)

This may have been going on in military circles for years, but it became famous when Alexander Haig joined the Reagan administration. He was a truly gifted exponent of Military Classy, creating such gems as *deimplementationable* and *superpreponderationism*. I can't vouch for these at first hand; they were reported to me by a colleague who may be pulling my leg. It's hard to believe that such monstrosities ever issued from human lips.

Donald E. Westlake, the author of many splendid comic crime novels, had a wonderful dialogue (in *Why Me*) in which an FBI man illustrated Haigspeak in top form, with such words as purloinment for theft, groupage for group, potentialism for potential, transactage for transaction, coincidentalistic for coincidental, and intentionisms for intentions. The rule is simple: add as many syllables as you can squeeze in, and you'll sound authoritative. Recently I heard "degradadation" for "degradation." Only two letters, but it lends just that extra touch of Class.

Now a glance at perhaps the oldest form of Classyspeak, the Genteel or Refained variation. As with the Military, no one ever dies in Genteel circles: they pass away. Sometimes they have gone before. They are not dead people: they are Loved Ones. (I thought this was an invention of Evelyn Waugh's, but undertakers – who are among our most fluent users of Genteelspeak – actually refer to corpses as Loved Ones.) They deplore the word undertaker, preferring funeral director. No one ever dies or is buried in these circles. After they pass on, or away, or are deceased, they are interred or entombed.

Genteel-speak also requires that one never uses a monosyllable if a polysyllable can be found. The Genteel Classyspeaker doesn't live in a house; he resides there. He never buys anything; he purchases, or acquires it. He doesn't make things, he fabricates them. Nor does he do anything; he performs it. He can neither start nor stop: he initiates, and finalizes or terminates. There are no drugs in the lexicon of Genteel Classy: instead, there are chemotherapeutic agents. *Resonate* is very big in Genteel circles, as it is in the military; I'm not quite sure what it's supposed to mean . . . some thing like strike a chord, or produce a response? The dictionary definition isn't much use. It's one of those words which people start using, like parameters, without being sure of what they're talking about. *Ambience* is very classy right now, and is generally used instead of atmosphere: "The ambience of this restaurant is rather charming". It's derived from the adjective "ambient," for circling about, surrounding, encompassing, as in ambient air and ambient light, much favoured by John Milton. So your ambience is the surrounding area. *Venue* is Classy for place. Since it's the past participle of *venir*, French verb meaning to come, it's correctly used for a meeting-place, where people come together (esp. for a match or competition, says the *Shorter Oxford*). Its main use, before it became vogueish, was in fencing – an assault, attack, thrust, hit, and so on. However, I've heard it used where one normally might discuss a course of action, or a procedure, and all sorts of other crazy things.

Yet another current favourite is *exudate*, used in strange contexts which seem to have little to do with its actual meaning. It is a variant of "exude", which has rather crass associations, like sweating and

96

emitting smells. *Plethora* is also popular, although usually mispronounced; accent should be on the first syllable, not the second. "Before" and "after" have disappeared from the Genteel vocabulary, and have been replaced with "prior to" and "subsequent."

"Ilk" is among the classiest of current words, occurring in almost all areas, but particularly in Military and Genteel circles. (Curious how often these two cross, though one would think they had little in common.) But Ilk crops up everywhere, universally misused; I recently heard some musical groups referred to as "three ilks". The intention was facetious, and God knows what the lady thought she was saying. Fowler and the *Shorter Oxford* say that ilk simply means *the same*. I'll quote Fowler:

> It does not mean family or kind or set or name. *Of that ilk* is a form constructed for the case in which proprietor and property have the same name: *the Knockwinnocks of that ilk* means the Knockwinnocks of Knockwinnock. The common maltreatments of the phrase . . . are partly unconscious and due to ignorance of the meaning of *ilk* and partly facetious; indulgence in such WORN-OUT HUMOUR is much less forgivable than for an English man not to know what a Scottish word means . . . (p.265)

That's telling 'em, H.W.!

The serious student of Genteel/Refained should look up Nancy Mitford's *Noblesse Oblige* which, although a trifle dated, is not only instructive on the linguistic level, but is also a valuable study of snobbery, both conscious and unconscious. Nancy mocked and condemned snobbery in others, but was herself a terrible snob. Language and snobbery are inextricably involved with one another; as Shaw remarked, it is impossible for an Englishman to open his mouth without making some other Englishman despise him.

The feminist movement has had some curious effects on English. Although in most respects, I am supportive of feminism, I find it impossible to go along with their language campaign. Words like mankind don't give me any trouble; surely they can be used inclusively to take in females as well as males? The word that turned me off the whole thing was "herstory", which kept cropping up at a conference, purporting to correct the injustice of "history". They may not all have been guilty, but at least one of the speakers thought that it literally meant "his story."

If feminists want to be taken seriously, they must do better than that. History comes from the Latin *historia* (same word in Greek) meaning "learning or knowing by inquiry, narrative, history; *histor* means knowing, learned, wise". I don't know any Greek, and I've forgotten most of my Latin, except for a few tags, but you can find all these useful things in a dictionary of etymology, and often in an ordinary dictionary.

There have been arguments over such ludicrous matters as whether "manhole" should be changed to something non-sexist: are we really going to waste time and space on such idiocies? Men are welcome to those holes in the road, as far as most of us are concerned, and everyone knows what the word means.

The manhole controversy is nothing compared to the wrangling over chairman. Does it really matter? And if it does, why can't we just say chairwoman? Some groups have compromised by describing the Chair's occupant as "the chair"; is it worse to be called a chairman than to be called a chair, which is an inanimate object with no brains and no gender? Must we interminably repeat he/she, or fall back on the ungrammatical "their", rather than use the convenient and conventional "he" as an inclusive pronoun? I find it very distracting and annoying. And a nuisance.

It's such a teapot-tempest. If one is concerned with writing or discussing a serious issue, surely the main objective is to communicate what one has to say, rather than having to stop at every sentence to worry about whether one is using sexist terminology? I am far more offended by a hideous neologism like "herstory" than I am by a poor old manhole. What do francophile feminists do with this dilemma? The gender of French nouns has no logic whatsoever. A French chair (chaise) is feminine, but an armchair (fauteuil) is masculine. Chairman (Président) is masculine, but chairmanship (présidence) is feminine.

Time and energy can be put to better use on real issues, rather than on this silly stuff. Let's get to work on equal pay for equal work, and put a stop to sexual molestation, instead of wasting time on herstory.

18

The Naughty Bits

There is nothing new about the Classy syndrome. Mrs. Malaprop and Dogberry are familiar figures, and in a way they're rather touching. They are trying to sound superior, to give the impression of being upper class, by using pretentious language. They desert familiar country to venture into the land-mined territory of polysyllables. It never works, and it has afforded writers great material for comedy. They were early exemplars of the Classy syndrome.

The world used to laugh at them. Now we pick up on their barbarisms, and incorporate them in our vocabulary. Mrs. Malaprop, not Shaw or Shakespeare or Churchill, has become our model and guide.

There is another trend in English, however, which I suspect is new, although equally undesirable. In the past, the deprived classes invariably tried to imitate the privileged – in dress, in speech, in manners. Some time in the Sixties a reverse process suddenly manifested itself – something, I believe, quite new, unless you count Marie Antoinette pretending to be a milkmaid. This was the adoption by the literate and intelligent, who should have known better, of lower-class language, gutter speech. This is not snobbery on my part and I make no apology for characterizing foul language as lower class. I don't mean "class" as defined by money, or titles, or any of the snob-indicators. If you can't speak a simple sentence without a lot of crude and offensive expressions, you're lower class in my book. Disgusting language is frequently used by the wealthy and privileged, but it's still a sign of inferiority.

In that unusual decade (Sixties, in case I lost you), along with confused ideas of liberation and equality, there occurred an equally confused idea that there was something more fundamentally virtuous about four-letter words than about socially acceptable equivalents. Many an eloquent article was written, particularly in student newspapers, extolling the "honesty" of saying *shit*. Rejection of that malodorous monosyllable has been attributed to hypocrisy, mealy-mouthery, and pseudo-gentility. In fact, the history of language shows a continual search for "polite" terms for smelly processes, each one in turn taking on the infection of the subject and falling into disrepute. Toilet, for example, was once a polite term which is now suppressed in favour of bathroom. A small girl of my acquaintance recently gave her mother a bottle of bathroom water as a birthday present – because toilet water sounded rude.

People have always sought, at least for use in social situations, substitute words for excreta and the less savoury physical processes not out of false gentility but because most of us don't particularly want to be reminded unnecessarily of urine, feces, and so on.

Shit, its champions to the contrary, has never been a socially acceptable word, nor has fuck. There was much bellowing of both these words at a poetry reading which I reluctantly attended; the reader prided himself on his Elizabethan lust for life, and what he called his Rabelaisan enjoyment of Reality. He said that "fuck" was a good old Anglo-Saxon word, but it isn't. It didn't come into the language until the 16th century, and was never accepted in decent use. "Origin unknown," says the *Concise Oxford*; my other dictionaries ignore it. Shit is Middle English, but it was agricultural, used of diarrhoea in farm animals. Not words for pleasant social occasions at all.

Rejection of such language is not Victorian prudery. Shakespeare and Chaucer made their lower-class characters vulgar enough, but neither of those words occur in their writing. Chaucer used *swyve* for the sex act, and Shakespeare used *tup*. As far as I can discover, they simply avoided the subject of bowel evacuation: after all, who wants to hear about that? It's not an amusing or interesting subject, except among the pre-school set where it is a favourite joke. Historically these have always been gutter words, used freely only by those who were not restrained by any delicacy of upbringing, or who simply didn't know better – whose vocabulary offered no alternatives.

The gutter words now dominate our language, and are in a fair way to extinguish all other vocabulary. The words have lost all meaning, and no longer have the smallest value for emphasis; they are used as sloppily and pointlessly by the literate as by the dirtiest-mouthed little boy in the slums.

Kingsley Amis's character Jake (in *Jake's Thing*) is pissed i.e., drunk. He is also pissed off, meaning that he is angry. Why this linguistic parsimony, making one (inappropriate) word work so hard? Another Amis, Martin, uses "fuck" so monotonously and indiscriminately that one begins to suspect he is simply suffering from an impoverished vocabulary and a paucity of imagination. Its use tells us nothing of the character of the speaker, since everyone in the book talks the same imprecise, unimaginative argot, a dreary repetition of fuck, shit, piss, ass-hole. Perhaps I do him an injustice, since I didn't finish reading the book; it may have ended with the non-hero meeting a pure and lovely girl with a thesaurus, and learning some new words. But I got too nawshus to go on.

Almost everyone says shit nowadays (except me, of course) and fart, and turd. I don't want to talk about excrement all the time, I don't want to think about it or listen to it. When you have small children, you have to deal with it, but it is never either an interesting nor an attractive subject for general conversation. Nevertheless it currently dominates most conversations.

"I just came by to pick up my shit," a young woman friend said, dropping in one afternoon. I blenched at the suggestion, but what she had really come to pick up was her laundry. Her washing machine had broken down, and she had used mine. But why call it shit, for goodness' sake? What's wrong with saying laundry, washing, my clean clothes?

I can't give the proper attribution to the next item, because I heard it at second-hand, but it illustrates the meaningless use of the word. A lady got off the bus, and cried out in dismay, "Oh, shit! I stepped in some doggy doo-doo!" That is, she used the word as an expletive, but avoided its literal application.

"He's *such* an ass-hole," a young man told me, affectionately, of his dog. He actually named the poor dog Ass-hole. I said this was a rotten thing to do to a dog, and spoke forcefully on the subject. The dog-owner was taken aback.

"I didn't mean a real ass-hole," he said defensively. He meant that the dog was puppyish, clownish. So why in heaven's name inflict that opprobrious appellation on a nice little animal? He simply had never thought of the real meaning of what he was saying.

Ass-hole is also used to mean a funny, clownish person: "You gotta hear this guy, he's a real ass-hole." (Of a comedian.)

If he is, I don't want to hear him. I object to the use of *ass* for the buttocks. There are plenty of words for that part of the anatomy – you can call it the bottom, the bum, the seat, the rear, the derrière – there's no shortage. Why introduce the quite irrelevant *ass*? It means a donkey, and was used facetiously for someone stupid or stubborn. "You silly ass!" Tinkerbell shrieked at Peter Pan. It's now a spoiled word, like *gay*, unusable in the former context. Its misuse in this context may be the result of a corruption of the British *arse*.

The prize exhibit is, of course, *fuck*. It used to be the ultimate Bad Word – for something so abominable that all other words were inadequate. Now it is the universal word, indiscriminately applied in any and every circumstance, and personally I'm terribly sick of it. I once forbade students in my writing class to use it; they had to improve their vocabularies, and this was impossible if they fell back in every sentence on fuck. This meant that some of them were left completely speechless; I was cajoled at last into making a concession. Everyone who completed all his assignments was allowed, once, to use fuck and shit before the Christmas exam. But they had to be used discriminatingly, and with effect. It was as if I had required them to wear muzzles, so effectually were they silenced by the loss of their only words.

It is not easy to make students believe such matters are important when Top Writers set them such poor examples. Here is Kingsley Amis's little boy Martin at work:

> It's easy to see what fucked me up . . . my mad fuck of a father killed my sister . . . Someone fucked up. Who the fuck are they, anyway, that they won't fuck me? What made them fuck me before? What is it with you fucking girls all of a sudden? . . . Fucking get up or get out, you fuck –

I forget the title of that masterpiece, but I remember reading a review that praised the dialogue. So authentic. Well, some people do talk like that. Some time ago I heard a motorist describing how he happened to get in an accident. In tones of bitter injury, he regaled us with the following:

Well, it wasn't *my* fucking fault. Fuck! This fucker came fucking out of the fucking access road, and cut right across my fucking lane, I never had a fucking chance. Fuck! Five hundred fucking bucks damage, and I gotta get a fucking lawyer . . .

And so on. But is it really the stuff of literature? Should he be praised for his vivid and lively dialogue, as Amis Jr. was?

When I refused to allow my students to rely on the four-letters for all purposes, they immediately assumed that I was shocked by such forthrightness. In fact, if I were going to be shocked by those words I would have been dead long since. I had to listen to them all day and every day in the college; they confronted me everywhere in graffitti and even in (alleged) literature. Constant repetition has robbed them of shock value – of any value. They have become mere noises, as meaningless as *like, y'know, basically.*

When fuck ceased to have shock-value, a new dimension of nastiness was provided by "motherfucker", on which many stand-up comedians rely for reflex laughs. My editor says that it is now mandatory in rock lyrics and videos, and is showing up in films, plays, and inevitably – literature. Of a sort.

There seems to be a strong belief among literary critics that there is some kind of intrinsic virtue in four-letter words. This may be a hangover from the days when D. H. Lawrence and James Joyce insisted on their right to use whatever language they chose, if it suited their purpose, and Lawrence made history when "fuck" appeared in print, in *Lady Chatterley's Lover.* The book was banned, there were great campaigns for the artist's right to free speech, and so on. I'm not arguing against that. I don't think any words should be banned, as such, but I think they should be used discriminatingly, judiciously; no word should be used as ubiquitously and pointlessly as fuck is in the foregoing examples.

Because Lawrence was an officially Great Writer, and because he used four-letter words, some critics immediately made the quite unjustified equation: Dirty words = Great Literature. As a result, it now appears that you can set up as a Great Writer if you just work in enough four-letters – a really easy way to achieve greatness. Actually *Lady Chatterley's Lover* is a pretty stupid book. I picked it up recently, and glanced through. I doubt if it would have even a faint chance of getting published today, without the warranty of a famous name. It's full of feeble snobbism, some really lousy dialogue, and social issues that are simply silly. I find it difficult to believe that the sorrows of Lady Chatterley and her gamekeeper were of much importance when the book was first published; Lawrence was an inverted snob, and the novel is full of embarrassing fantasizing. The sensation it caused was attributable to the novelty of seeing those bad words in print, not to any intrinsic literary qualities.

Writing of this type has been designated by Mimi Kramer, in a *New Yorker* theatre review, as "artsy-dirty". She notes astutely that it's all phoney, the characters ". . . waxing alternately pseudo-lyrical about sex and pseudo-crude about their bodily functions, spitting and scratching their crotches a lot, in the service of establishing the play's status as Serious Theatre." (May 15 '91, p. 94.)

This becomes entangled (particularly among male writers) with another rather depressing tendency: poorly concealed sexual bragging. "God, but I'm a wild, erotic stud," the author is unsubtly telling his readers. This has been recently manifested in long, disgusting passages (artsy-dirty, pseudo-erotic) as follows:

"God, he loved her ass," writes a male producer of crime novels. He is fantasizing about his deceased wife, in a passage with absolutely no relevance to the plot. ". . . watching his own head buried between her legs, tasting her, smelling her, feeling her wonderful firm and soft ass in both grasping palms . . ."

There is a full page of this, but instead of erotic, I find it offputting in the extreme. If I were his wife, I'd divorce him on the strength of that passage alone. Is *nothing* private?

The description in careful detail of sexual encounters is mandatory in contemporary novels. Now the sex act, when one is one's self involved in it, is absorbing to the exclusion of everything else. Second-hand, however, it is apt to be tedious, if not offputting. I've often been glad, reading the excruciating accounts of so-called lovemaking in books, or watching them on television, that I was brought up in an unenlightened, repressed age; otherwise I might have been put off sex altogether by the unappetizing representations. It was reassuring to find an up-to-date novelist supporting me in this belief.

Novelists, when their characters drive cars, never feel compelled to describe precisely what the physical actions are of hands, feet, eyes, knees, elbows. Yet many of these same novelists, when their characters copulate, get into such detailed physical descriptions you'd think they were writing an exercise book. We all know the inter-relation between the right ankle and the accelerator when driving a car, and we needn't be told. In sex we all know about knees, thighs, fingers, the softness at the side of the throat, here-let-me-help, how's that, *mf, mf, mf.* And if you don't know it, you shouldn't read dirty books anyway; they'll only give you the wrong idea. – Donald C. Westlake, *Dancing Aztecs*, p. 336.

And a writer from an earlier generation gives a character this astute comment:

". . . sex-starved people are immensely preoccupied with sex. Much cry, little wool! I always suspect people who boast of their rich and various sexual experiences. I find myself doubting if they ever had any, worth speaking of. Satisfied people hold their tongues. They know it's an unlucky subject to discuss . . . Terribly unlucky. When Psyche turned on the light, Eros flew out of the window. He's a very touchy god and he can't bear publicity. And that," he said to the three young men, "is why you boys will never be able to pick up much information at second hand. Those who know won't talk. Those who talk don't know." – Margaret Kennedy, *The Feast*, p. 123.

I wish some editors and producers and critics would reflect on that; I've so often been adjured to "let it all hang out . . ." Not to be afraid of reality, which seems to mean sex scenes. (Otherwise the book won't sell.) They seem genuinely to believe that we all have insatiable appetites for watching or reading exercise books about people rolling around with no clothes on . . .

Much cry, little wool, ladies and gentlemen.

It was disappointing to find that Donald Westlake in a later book forgot his own good advice, and (instead of being funny, at which he's an expert) inflicted on his reader a good many descriptions of not very interesting copulations, and details such as "She felt his come run down her leg." Who cares? I've been a devoted Westlake fan for years, but I never finished that book. I could transcend the over-abundant sex scenes, or simply skip, but it had none of the pace and wit of his others. What could have happened to him, I wondered, dismayed. Could his marriage have broken up, forcing him into these dreary fantasies? But then I reflected that it was probably his publishers, insisting that he practise realism, let it all hang out, et cetera. It should be noted that in an earlier book, *Good*

Behaviour, he used fuck with such brilliant comic effect that I fell on the floor laughing.

However, this variety of comedy requires great skill. There is a quite unwarranted belief among stand-up comedians that there is something intrinsically funny about four-letter words. I once sat numbly through an allegedly comic routine which relied entirely on this principle. "Fuck," he would say. "Shit. Laugh, you fuckers." And the audience would dutifully produce a laugh, for fear they might be considered prudish, or lacking in a sense of humour.

Here's an illustration from a murder mystery, which was in some respects an interesting book, with a vivid background in archaeology and physics, about which the author seemed to be well informed. It was constantly interrupted with painfully explicit descriptions of the heroine's sexual adventures; recently widowed, she was "horny." But women can't be horny; they have no horn. They can be sexually aroused, or sex-starved, or libidinous, or passionate, or even hot. Try Roget.

Every detail was painstakingly dwelt upon, invariably with a careful explanation of how the lady got out of her underwear. Oh, for heaven's sake! Do we really have to be instructed in these adolescent preoccupations? The plot was slowed by these incidents, and I found myself getting heartily sick of the heroine's itch.

Rather late in the book we meet a heroic figure – a detective-cum-archaeologist, a wise and gentle man of great intelligence and perspicacity, who solves the mystery. Now listen to the internal monologue of this Renaissance man:

> Why the fuck was he now on his way to Cambridge with this cop to bust some turd who got sick of playing spy . . . The guy must be a total ass-hole . . .

Can we go on believing in our hero's intellectual integrity after that? I've spent a good part of my life in academic circles, and I don't believe serious scholars think in four-letter words, like dirty-minded pre-adolescents. They have to have better vocabularies to survive professionally.

Most children go through foul-mouth phases: there's the nursery stage summed up in the Flanders and Swan song – "Pee, poo, belly, bum, drawers," though even in the nursery set, that would be tame stuff nowadays.

Later – I'm not sure of the age, early adolescence? – there is another stage in which most of us try to prove ourselves by smoking, using bad language, experimenting with drugs. The heavy peer pressure stage. Prior to the language revolution of the Sixties, girls ("nice girls") grew out of this quite soon: it was kid stuff, eliciting no response but a languidly lifted eyebrow. Boys – I gather – continued to use it among themselves for life, but NOT in mixed company.

I clearly remember the first time in adult life that I actually heard the word fuck spoken in public. We were sitting on the verandah of a summer hotel, having a drink after a swim, when a drunk man staggered out, yelling and cursing. We ignored him, but finally he spoke the forbidden word.

"Hey," said one of our young men, "hey, fella – ladies present." He went on yelling *the word*, and the boys rose as one and threw him out. It was simply inadmissible. I must admit I feel a certain nostalgia for those long-lost times.

When I was about eight, I was severely punished for saying shit, which I had heard on the lips of the mother of a school-friend; I thought this adult use made it acceptable. I trotted home and immediately tried it out on the family, with dreadful results.

"Mrs. Thing said it," I protested, in self-defence, and my mother said coldly that Mrs. Thing was not to be taken as a model.

"We don't talk like people who are less fortunate than ourselves," said Maw superbly.

This was puzzling, because the Things lived in a bigger house than we did, had a car – which we didn't – and in all external things seemed more fortunate than we were. (But nothing was paid for.)

Nevertheless, I have since acknowledged the justice of my mama's claim. If they are reduced to expressing every experience, every emotion, through a vocabulary restricted to shit, piss, fuck, asshole, then they are in fact less fortunate than those of us with a more flexible command of language. They're deprived, lower-class, non-U, poor and ignorant.

Why the rest of us, who know better, should feel obliged to imitate them, impoverishing (in the name of some feeble theory of honesty or equality or classlessness) our own more privileged vocabularies, I for one can't see. Even if I end up with no one to talk to.

However, I probably will always have a few people to converse with, for a rather odd reason. Many of those rebels against convention, those defenders of the use of four-letter words, have long out-grown the defiant stage. They've settled down, got married, and started to bring up families. It is startling to observe the change in their attitude toward language. They have suddenly become proper, even prissy. They don't want their kids using vulgarities.

Asses have suddenly become bottoms, and ass-holes are unmentionable. The four-letters are not allowed in the house. Of course the kids use them among their peers, but they thoughtfully make an effort not to let their parents know that they know them. They pretend to be shocked when the words are used in their parents' hearing.

A six-year-old friend was telling me recently about a bad kid in his class. This monster did not brush his teeth, he threw gum-wrappers on the street, he told lies, and – said my friend, lowering his voice piously and frowning disapprovingly – "He says fuck." Now I had heard my informant using this and other rude words with great freedom and at the top of his lungs while playing with his little friends; but convention demands that innocent adults be spared the knowledge.

This seems to be a general pattern, except in the field of literature and entertainment, where it is still considered advanced, and significant, and essential to realistic effects, to lard every sentence with these rather tedious expressions. No doubt some time art will catch up with life, and fictional characters will be allowed to make a few remarks without the mandatory fuck, shit, piss or ass-hole. I hope I live long enough to see it.

My final argument, or plea, or protest, is by no means original with me. Many other plaintive voices have raised the same objection. Fuck is supposed to mean the sex act. It presumably refers to love making: the most intimate, warm, tender relationship possible between two people. It is, nevertheless, an abuse word, the ultimate obscenity. Of course its erstwhile force has been lost with its forbidden quality: overuse has destroyed its shock potential, but it is still intended abusively, contemptuously, hatefully.

What does this say about our society, and our attitude to sex? Why do we allow this ugly word to be used as a synonym for love? Do we really think sex is contemptible and obscene? That passage from Martin Amis's book reveals something horrible about the author's attitude toward women and sex, when he uses the same word for the act of love and as an expression of loathing and anger.

At least some of this attitude has been inculcated by religion. Fertility was honoured and praised in the very early religions, but modern ones have historically despised and distrusted women as sexual creatures, honouring them only as perennial virgins, sworn to chastity. They are reluctantly tolerated as mothers, but are constantly reminded that children are begotten in Sin. It is this kind of male chauvinist piggery that has turned love-making into fucking.

Language affects thought, and thought affects behaviour. The wrong language makes enemies of men and women. Instead of being lovers they become violators and victims. That's why we can't ignore the corruption of language, or pretend that it's of no importance. It must be continually publicly attacked.

CHAPTER

19

The Ed Biz

A faculty meeting was discussing a student whose family suffered from education snobbery. It was imperative that their son attend university, that everyone in their family attend university. Sad to say, this unfortunate kid wasn't going to make it through Grade 13 – unless the family succeeding in blackmailing and bullying the school into raising his marks. Everyone agreed that we couldn't do it.

"He'll just have to go to Teachers' College," was the final verdict of the chairperson. "He can teach public school."

This was in the dim past, before the days when all teachers were required to have a university degree.

This decision exposes the root cause of trouble in our education system. There is still a lingering belief that any half-wit is good enough to teach public school (or high school English), whereas only the best and brightest are fit to teach in post-secondary institutions.

Such a view betrays a deplorable sense of values. The best and brightest should be in the public schools, getting kids off on the right foot, so that they are well-grounded in essentials, and enjoy school. Public school teachers should be the most highly paid in the system, should have small classes (ideally, twelve to fifteen in the early grades, no more than twenty at any level) and should not be run ragged with overwork. Conditions should be such that they will love their work, enjoy every minute of it, so they will establish happy relationships with the kids, and will feel the enthusiasm and dedication that is indispensable for teaching and learning. They must, of course, know their subjects thoroughly and be experts in their fields.

In Grades One to Three, efforts have been made to keep classes small (although most are still over twenty), but thereafter teachers are still facing crowded classrooms and associated discipline problems. Large numbers and discipline problems are invariably associated.

Under our present system, public school teachers work longer hours, have larger classes, and are accorded less prestige than teachers in any other part of the system. They are overworked and overtired. Burn-out is pervasive. The effect on kids of discouraged and exhausted teachers is drastic. Not much learning goes on in such conditions. That's one of the reasons that people can go right through the system without learning to read, much less mastering grammar and spelling, math and history and geography.

The suggestion that we should cut class size and insist on a low pupil/teacher ratio inevitably elicits the same response: it is too expensive. The taxpayer can't afford it.

A few years ago, it was discovered that millions in government grants had been given to strip clubs. We regularly spend in the neighbourhood of twelve billion annually on so-called "defence", and of course we can always afford a war: there are big profits for arms manufacturers in a nice war, preferably in some remote part of the world where the environmental damage won't affect us immediately. We spend millions on such cosmetic appointments as governor-general, on outrageous travel expenses and limos for politicians, on a completely unnecessary office for the Prime Minister's wife, on redecorating official residences, on filling the patronage trough to reward the P.M.'s buddies. The office of the governor-general is supposed to lend dignity and prestige to official occasions, but the sight of Ray Hnatyshyn looking like the Mad Hatter, and speaking French so dreadful as to cause toothache, did not produce that effect. We can afford all this stuff, but we haven't enough money to make the education system work.

The general public has an idea that teachers spend fifteen-odd hours in classes, and have the rest of the week to loaf around smoking pot and molesting students. Let me state, as temperately as possible that this view is inaccurate. Let us concede that a good knowledge of English (including reading, writing, spelling, grammar, et

111

al.) is fundamental: without competence in reading and writing, all other subjects are closed to us. If you want students to graduate with adequate skills, they have to practise those skills: they have to write sentences and paragraphs and essays continually, and the teacher has to mark them.

For most of my teaching career, I had five (sometimes six) classes of three hours each, weekly; with between 30 and 40 per class, this meant at minimum of 150 students. If they wrote 1500 words a month each, and allowing 15 minutes per paper for corrections and comments, that meant about 40 hours of marking. If any individual consultation were to be given – say 10 minutes a week, which isn't nearly enough – that was another 25 hours, or a rough total of eighty hours a week, without allowing for lesson preparation, and helping with the drama club, let alone finding time for my own child and running the house.

Obviously no one can keep this up without going cuckoo, and I cut down where I could: on marking, on individual assistance. I knew the kids weren't getting the help they needed, but if I tried to do the job right, I would end up in the bin, which wouldn't help anyone much.

If I could have worked a forty-hour week, I could have done a good job, and enjoyed it. But the eighty-hour week is Burnoutsville, and even the most conscientious teachers are driven to scamping their work, and eventually to quit caring. But if you suggest small classes as a solution, with the inevitable increase in cost, taxpayers froth at the mouth.

I remember one theorist, who had obviously never soiled his hands with chalk in his life, announcing that it was just as easy to teach 200 people as it was to teach 20. He obviously thought that teaching meant standing in front of a lectern, delivering a lecture, and then going out to play golf. Or smoke pot, or molest little girls, or whatever teachers do in their free time. (Most of us mark papers.) If I had had a rotten egg or a tomato on me at the time, that theorist would have got it right in the mush. But there – you never have these things when you need them.

High school teaching offers slightly smaller classes, a shorter year, and more prestige than public school teachers enjoy. Post second-ary education is still easier and pleasanter. It's still hard work, and classes are frequently far too large, but you're dealing with adults, most of the problem students are long gone, and the teaching year is two months shorter. Professors in graduate schools often have classes with eight or ten students, marvellously light time-tables, and a six-month academic year. They have – comparatively – enormous prestige, not always deserved. They will argue that their burden is no less heavy than those at other levels: one of them told me about the terrible demands made on his time by meetings. Apparently they believe that teachers at other levels of education don't have meetings. In one high school where I taught, we were trying to develop a team-teaching project; we had a meeting *every night* in the first term.

I've never taught public school, but I know that most high school teachers can plan on a minimum of 150 students annually.

Further, in university, a good deal of the dog-work – essay and examination marking – is done by serfs, little troops of Sidney Carton-like "jackals" who in my day were allotted for their work a freezing room with a few battered tables and chairs and one bare light bulb.

"Doth God exact day-labour, light denied?" queried a plaintive legend on the wall, underneath which someone else had written the succinct response, "Yes."

Professors also protest about the demands on them for great scholarship, constant study: don't give me that, guys. That's a privilege, and if you don't want to do it, you don't have to. It's the sort of thing the rest of us do for enjoyment, in our spare time. They are also under heavy pressure to publish. Oh, how sad! When I was teaching high school, I wrote regularly for education journals, as well as for the gutter press (*Saturday Night*, *Chatelaine*, *Canadian Forum*, *This Magazine*, eck cetera). Instead of thinking of it as a burden, I thought I was lucky to get in print. Much of the stuff published by English faculty belongs on that little list of things that never would be missed, and is read by an audience so small as to be nearly invisible.

The thinking behind this system is that teaching at such exalted levels demands great scholarship and intellect, and so the teachers must be given lots of liberty and high rewards. Nevertheless, professors are often extraordinarily bad teachers. I spent four years in graduate schools (not counting extra-mural course-taking) and most of the courses were quite remarkably bad – far inferior to undergraduate courses. Only one of my graduate instructors knew anything about how to teach (and he was in Modern Languages, not English) and the atmosphere in the lecture halls and seminar rooms was often disagreeable – a kind of all-pervading snobbishness, with unconcealed contempt for students, those tiresome creatures who cluttered lecture rooms and usurped the valuable time of the Great Mind, impatient to be set free to write literary criticism.

While students were needed in the classrooms, where they were necessary for justifying education appropriations, they were not wanted by graduate school faculties. I had been encouraged to return and work on my doctorate; I was even given grants and awards, and it was a shock to find that instead of being a deserving person of high potential value, I was a tiresome nuisance.

Since I'd quit a job, and had been persuaded to switch from the Fourth Estate to Academe, it was disturbing to be sneered at, ignored, and addressed with withering contempt, as if I were feeble-minded. I began to wonder if indeed I might be feeble-minded. In one course, the professors (there were two of them, collaborating) despised the class so much that no one dared to ask a question, except for a few longstanding buddies who had been with them as undergraduates.

"There are too many Ph.D. candidates in English," snarled one graduate school instructor. "It shouldn't be allowed. They have to be weeded out."

Although I wasn't exactly weeded out, I eventually decided that enough time had been wasted; my doctoral dissertation will never be be written. For one thing, any thesis topic that I found interesting was rejected as "not scholarly"; real scholarship seemed to be identified with footnotes and pedantry. I also ran out of money. All of this, of course, will no doubt be written off as sour grapes, the puckered mouth of someone who couldn't stand the pace. It isn't true, but I'll never be able to prove it. The point of reviving these painful memories is that our education system is upside down, with prestige, power, and financial rewards at the wrong end.

If public school teachers were given anything approximately as pleasant as the working conditions we give to university teachers, we would graduate an enormously improved product, and would attract the best people to the field.

A prerequisite for successful teaching in the early stages is small classes. At university level discipline has ceased to be an issue, but from Grades Six to Eleven, it's *the* problem. On my first day of teaching, I walked into a room with thirty-five seats and forty kids; the noise was like a battlefield. Every year we were lured with promises of small classes; every year the numbers increased.

Teaching young children so that they don't form bad habits that persist for life requires a lot of individual attention. When my son was in Grade I, there were forty-odd kids in the class; the school week consisted of 25 classroom hours. That is, if the teacher gave each child seven and a half minutes of individual attention each day, she would have no time for anything else at all. This is bad enough with older groups, but with young children it's disastrous.

Nowadays, in favoured areas, I believe classes are smaller, but they tend to keep gradually edging up and up, particularly when education appropriations are being systematically eroded by the policies of the federal government. When I first went to teach in a community college, the policy was to have no classes with more than twenty students. In my last year, I had several mobs of thirty-five and forty.

If we could start children off enjoying school and developing real pleasure in learning, so that they have mastered the fundamentals before they get into high school, we wouldn't have to spend fortunes on remedial classes. Kids would be self-motivating, and by senior high school would probably need little more than direction. If you have ever taught a class like this – and I had a couple during my years in the wilderness – you'll know that it's pure joy. If I could have afforded it, I'd have done it for nothing. All the teacher had to do was throw them an idea, and they were off and running. They may not have been any brighter, as far as IQ measurements go, than any other group of senior high schoolers, but they'd been lucky in having good teachers, and at home a climate favourable to education. They'd discovered that learning could be wild fun.

My Grade 13 class decided that *in addition* to the regular curriculum, they would do a production of *The Importance of Being Earnest* – just to see what it was like. They made their own costumes and scenery, they stayed for hours after school, and they had a hilarious time, as well as learning a great deal about Oscar Wilde and the thinking of his period. The teachers involved had just as much fun as the kids. This kind of thing, I submit, is what education is all about.

Here's my recipe: Spend the money on the early years, on the best and most ideal conditions in public school. Don't grudge money to public school teachers, and try to wring every drop of blood out of them, in the hope of getting your money's worth. You'll get it all back with interest in the later years, and we'll be able to graduate literate students who can use language and other skills to realize their full potential as human beings.

Of course we need good teachers at all levels of education, and we should treat them generously, and not overload them with work so that they're exhausted and hostile. But it's far more important at the early stages than at the later.

As students master the necessary fundamentals, they develop the skills for learning independently, and by the time they're in university they will be able to work independently, with constructive direction from professors.

A few years ago, I re-read Washington Irving's "Legend of Sleepy Hollow", and was struck by the contempt accorded school teachers. It's everywhere in 19th century literature. Dickens' school teachers are a mixed lot of brutes and incompetents; the occasional capable and decent young man soon gets out of the racket. Jane Fairfax, in *Emma* contemplated life as a governess, in which she would "retire from all the pleasures of life, of rational intercourse, equal society, peace and hope, to penance and mortification forever."

Teachers were despised because, for all their education, they were poor. Nonetheless, their miserable salaries were angrily begrudged. I don't know how often I've listened to fulminations against the huge salaries paid to teachers, with their easy hours, their long holidays, their presumption in expecting to be paid a living wage.

I knew a man who ran for the school board with one object in life – to punish teachers. His attitude toward them could only be described as hatred. Predictably, teachers in his jurisdiction quit their jobs, and the area got such a bad reputation that they began to have difficulties in attracting anyone to their schools. This only inflamed his rage (it proved how irresponsible and unreliable teachers were) and he never once connected their problems with his attitude and influence.

A great many people hate and resent teachers, some of them with justice, for teachers (frequently when they've endured years of overwork and humiliation) sometimes get nasty. Some of them should never be in the field to begin with. But nowadays there is a strong conviction that teachers *owe* students a credit, whether or not they do any work, or are exposed as cheats.

I once had a student who asked if he could write short stories instead of critical essays; his bent was for creativity, not criticism. He submitted, as his own work, a section from *Three Men in a Boat*. When I pointed out that it was a poor choice, for the purposes of deception, since the chance of a teacher recognizing it was high, he refused absolutely to admit that he had stolen it. However, he gave some thought to sources with which English teachers might be unfamiliar and handed in a story from *Playboy's Stories for Swinging Readers*. Copied word for word. It was a clever story, and I'd been using it in my writing classes to teach plot structure.

In spite of all this, he swore up and down that he had written the story himself. Years later I bumped into this young man one day, and he still bore a grudge against me for failing him. He railed and stormed at me for several minutes. In self-defence, I pointed out the facts of the short story incident.

"That was a damned good story!" he bellowed, and so it was.

"But *you* didn't write it," I pointed out. "You stole it."

Do you know, he still wouldn't admit it? I don't understand this mind-set at all, but there is some kind of belief that teachers have an obligation to pass students, no matter how incompetent their work, or how dishonest their practices. Another student presented me with one of those store-bought essays, easily recognizable as such, on *Macbeth*. I called her in and questioned her, and she not only had not read *Macbeth*, she hadn't even read the spurious essay. She didn't know who Duncan was, or Macduff, or Malcolm, though she did have a dim idea that there was this Lord Macbeth, and his wife, this Lady Macbeth.

She was indignant that I would not give her a credit, and complained about me to the Dean, who didn't know too much about *Macbeth* either. (You don't have to read a lot of boring plays to be dean of a big English department.)

It is interesting that, in our current ethical climate, no shame attaches to being caught cheating. At one time, the guilty party would have been crushed by the disgrace. Nowadays the store-bought essay seems in some circles to be acceptable as a valid education tool.

Students are understandably hostile when they pay good money for an essay, only to have it rejected on some petty ethical count.

The slovenliness of our language makes it easier for us to have foolish thoughts. I have been trying to suggest, in this chapter, the ways in which our education system contributes to the decay of English. It might be summed up as a poor sense of values.

Rescuing our language is not a task just for schools and colleges and universities, nor just for the media, but for absolutely every one of us. We have to recognize its importance, not grudge paying for it, and be willing to work at it.

Is it really possible for students to get all the way to university without learning to spell or punctuate? I have before me a copy of *The Silhouette*, McMaster's student newspaper. The cut-line on a photo reads,

> Universities always complain they don't get enough funding . . . so they can open up the campus to students, make it more acessable [. . .] Every chance they get the administration puts up the detour sign . . . like in Mills library (above). But don't worry we're looking out for you!

The square brackets are mine, to indicate an omission. All those other dots are the writer's evasion of real punctuation. Commas are needed after "get" and "worry", and accessible needs another c, and an *ible* instead of that *able*. Right before their eyes, actually in their photograph, was a sign reading "Access Blocked", in front of a library where books would be available for checking spelling. They still managed to make two mistakes in one word. And these are would-be journalists, at university level.

20

Words and Music

A few years ago, the wife of American Senator Albert Gore launched a campaign against raunchy songs. It seems contemporary rock carries gruesome messages of violence, is sexually abusive and degrading to women. While deploring this, Mrs. Gore worried about censorship: the entertainment industry gets hostile at any suggestion that its "freedom" be limited, and this provokes anxiety in politicians. "Such criticism," observed the New York *Times*, "is not the sort of thing that gets entertainment dollars flowing." This is a sad reflection on our democratic processes: must we sacrifice conscience for fear of offending a possible source of support-dollars?

I used to have a dim idea that nobody really liked censorship, but recently it's become clear that certain religious communities are hungry to censor not only our reading and viewing, but our private lives. I'll fight it to the death. On the other hand – without censorship at some level, how can society control the ghouls who profit from the debasement of other humans? Are we left with a choice between draconic censorship and destructive exploitation of the innocent by some of the lowest vermin in existence? Kiddy-porn has to be the most depraved, the most abominable crime humanly conceivable.

However, I can't get worked up about song lyrics because I can't figure out how anyone knows what they are. Last fall I was taken to a concert in New York, and the music was so loud I couldn't hear it. The words were totally unintelligible. They may have been obscene and offensive, or possibly elevated and inspiring, but how could you tell? A few days later we went to a concert of ragtime music by a pianist-singer called Max Morath; he played and sang unamplified, and I could hear every word he said. The words were unexceptionable, but in the course of the programme, we were given a brief history of ragtime, and it was diverting to learn that, in its heyday, preachers thundered against it, condemning it as corrupting the morals of the youth of America. It's sad to think of all those young people now spending eternity in hell, because they listened to "Won't You Come Home, Bill Bailey?"

An acquaintance whose life was blighted by having a minister for a father once told me that his sermons, regardless of their ostensible text, used to slide into denunciations of the "crooners" of the thirties, whose warblings were specifically designed to entrap young girls into vice. That's what Rudy Vallee was up to, the old sex monster. Believe it or not, Bing Crosby – whom I've always thought of as a priestly pillar of righteousness – was considered a particularly insidious threat to female virtue.

Mrs. Gore suggested a law requiring that warning labels be placed on record sleeves and cassette and CD covers. Wrong, wrong, wrong! If you stick a label on a record – on *anything* – warning that it contains filthy language, and content that is sexually abusive and degrading to women, sales will rocket. Top of the charts with a bullet, as they say in the trade.

No, if you want to discourage kids from buying music, it's all right to stick on a label, but it should say, "This thoughtful and intelligent song has great educative and cultural value." No self-respecting child would be caught dead listening to it.

Serious collectors, I believe, carefully read descriptive literature about the music they buy. Does the average teenager read it, any more than he reads books or newspapers? Perhaps. And perhaps the kids are better than I am at interpreting the noises on records, or at concerts. I still suspect they would have to work like dogs, and dedicate hours of attention to interpreting the gibberish. Perhaps if they do, they will glean some disgusting language and references to sadistic practices. It's hard to imagine language very much filthier than the kids habitually use themselves, and unintelligibility may well defuse most of the destructive message.

I heard several excerpts from some of the songs currently in question (on "Think" programmes), and I couldn't distinguish a single word. Until the singers learn to enunciate a little better, and keep the background noise down a trifle, I suspect that society is fairly safe from this particular danger.

If we laugh tolerantly at the nasty stuff, dismissing it as unimportant, it loses its mystery. If we get feverishly alarmed and forbid it, or try to get it banned, the kids will lust to hear it, believing they are missing some kind of lubricious mystery.

The radio has just finished playing, as I write this, a song which seems to be called "Civilization". The words go as follows: "Civeelizay-shun. Civeelizay-shun. Civeelizay-shun. Civ . . ." Correction: not words, word. There's only one. I don't suppose it really lasted for fifteen minutes, but even two minutes of a one-word song begin to seem interminable.

After the final civeelizashun, there was some discussion in the studio of the song's meaning. I gathered that it was very significant, even though it had only one word. What the singer was doing was making the listener *think*. By hearing civeelizashun repeated several hundred times, the dimwitted listener would be forced into thinking about the corruptness of civilization. Well, doggone. What an insensitive clod I am; *I* thought that anyone who couldn't write better than that should get a job in a foundry. If the singer could do that with one word, think what he could convey with no words at all!

Can't we be persuaded to reflect on civilization without someone thumping the word incessantly in our ears? As I listened, I found myself irritably remembering a book by Freud called *Civilization and Its Discontents*, reflecting that one of my discontents is with one-word songs, and similar fakes, frauds, and put-ons. So perhaps it *did* make me think, after all – it's at least twenty years since I read that book.

This is not an indictment by the elderly of youth. If I'd really wanted to shut up "Ceeveelization", I could have turned off the radio. Perhaps I rather enjoyed thinking that I could write better words than that myself. My only real complaint against popular music is the volume; it hurts my ears. No matter what the era, the general run of songs is pretty awful, but in every period, every so often, along comes a melody to lift your spirit, and make you want to dance. The bad ones die and are forgotten; the good ones survive. When we look back, the past seems golden, because we only remember the best. Oddly enough, when one of those magical songs comes along, words and music are often equally pleasing: good music almost dictates good words.

Songs like "Civeelizashun" and the gruesome ones which are alarming Mrs. Gore quickly die a natural death, unless their lives are artificially prolonged by ill-advised publicity.

A friend tells me that she recently watched a "serious, adult programme" on Rap groups, in which the song words were unintelligible, but were printed on the screen as in simultaneous translations. They described every form of sexual perversion (bestiality, necrophilia, sado-masochism) in gutter language, and advocated gang-rape, torture, murder, and violence against women. Many people have protested against their concerts and albums, and needless to say, many others have sprung to their defence, in the interest of free speech.

There is no easy answer to this constantly recurring problem. Nevertheless, I suspect that censorship only gives the offenders publicity, on the old "banned in Boston" principle for guaranteeing a best seller. I still wonder whether the best approach wouldn't be to solemnly praise them, explaining that despite their salacious content, they are of serious sociological importance.

That would put off most teenagers, and it might even be true.

CHAPTER

21

In a Fine Frenzy

I had thought, tentatively, of writing a chapter on contemporary poetry, but disqualified myself on the grounds of incapacity. I can't seem to read the stuff. Luckily, a volunteer presented himself, one with high qualifications, if his resumé can be believed.

This volunteer, who claims to be himself a once-famous poet, has been living in my cellar. At one time his work was widely published, but by what he calls "accidents of birth", he lost touch with his editors and has been living obscurely in the shape of a silverfish (a small insect of sorts, in case you're not acquainted with silverfish). He has, in the face of unimaginable hardships, kept up with contemporary trends in poetry, through books and magazines stacked in the cellar. The silverfish dreams of being a librarian in his next incarnation: "Anything with hands."

To avoid misunderstanding, I might as well identify him: he is the reincarnation of Don Marquis's famous archy, a cockroach who lived in the Marquis garage, and wrote poetry (*the lives and times of archy and mehitabel*) by jumping on the typewriter keys. Since he couldn't jump on the shift key and a letter at the same time, all of his poetry was in lower-case; unwittingly, he influenced generations of lower-case poets, who thought that if lower-case made archy famous, it should do the same for them. (Same pattern as with four-letter words.) When will they learn that you can imitate form but you can't imitate genius?

archy redivivus has enlisted the help of a bookworm, who also makes claims to past greatness; he was once a book critic on the staff of the publisher of the Pogo comic books, where he was considered an authority on good taste in literature.

I was fortunate enough to get a brief interview with the two great minds one rainy Saturday, when I caught the silverfish in the throes of composition.

"Were you archy?" I asked, and he admitted it, shedding an infinitesimal tear, and speeding about on the computer keyboard.

im glad you invested in a computer, theres no way i could work a
typewriter   the shape im in now at least when i was a cockroach   i
could jump on the keys   being a silverfish is worse as far as poetry is
concerned

i seem to be going downhill on the evolutionary topography   and this
   bookworm doesnt know   from the industrial revolution   he keeps
 complaining that paper doesnt taste as good as parchment   still hes
got a few ideas which is more than i can say for most poets these days

worm and i dont agree on much but we have a consensus on this

if youre going to call it poetry   you gotta make it different from prose

 dont go jumping to conclusions   we arent naive Edgar Guest addicts
we think we shall never see   a poet as sick-making as joyce kilmer

but we insist there has to be   something to distinguish it from prose
   and it isnt enough to write it in uneven lines
      with no punctuation
or capital letters

i could have capitals nowadays   modern technology makes it easy
but i got in bad habits when i was a cockroach
i seem to think lower case if you know what i mean

that stuff i used to write wasnt real poetry   do you think i
      didnt know that interrogation point
it was a gag   but the dimbulb critics are so stupid
   theyll swallow anything   ha ha that's a joke for worm

okay worm – *some* of the dimbulb critics   not all   where was i
dimbulb critics   will swallow anything if its pretentious enough
   and gets a lot of promotion and publicity

for instance theyre now promoting something they call quote poetic
prose close quote or another quote prose poetry close quote

i say self-pity is bad art   axiomatically

poetic prose   is whitewash for selfindulgent crapiola   by someone
who is too lazy to do the hard work of constructing a novel   and
hasnt enough literary conscience to write a real poem   which is even
harder work   in fact writing a good poem may be the hardest work
   in the world

on the other hand theres nothing easier than writing phoney poetry
   which is usually bad prose in uneven lines
      with no punctuation
       and no capital letters
        and pretensions to profundity

what makes this stuff poetry i once asked a wasp that got into
   the cellar inadvertently   on a pear   he claimed to be a poet
      because his soul was elevated   by the sweet scent of pears

its the philosophic depth   said the wasp   its the vivid imagery
   you gotta have vivid imagery for poetry   said this wasp
   thats the sting in the tail

you can have vivid imagery in prose   the worm said   heres one from
   a detective story i just ate   i quote   he bounced around in the
      elevator like a neutrino in a lab experiment*

you better give a credit on that i said   make a footnote he said
and dont interrupt

i repeat   poetry has to be recognizably different from prose or why
do you call it poetry

its poetry because i say its poetry   because im a poet   and you
   better shut your head or youll feel the sting in my tail   the
      wasp said   im normally a vegetarian but i could change   if im
       still stuck in this cellar when the pears run out

hes only got one vivid image   the worm said to me aside   take away
   the sting in his tail and hes finished
the best way of showing whats wrong   with contemporary poetry is
   to print a sample poem and show whats wrong with it

   "I can't do that," I said, "I might get sued by some infuriated poet."

sued-shmued [wrote the silverfish] worm wanted to do something on
   concrete poetry   he says its the worst   its what bum poets write
      to conceal the poverty of their ideas   they think they can fool

   *donald c westlake, in good behaviour

125

people by messing around with typography   but after he ate a couple
  of concrete poems

he got such a case of indigestion he had to lay off criticism for
weeks   hes getting ready to pupate and thatll finish him as a critic
hell turn into a moth and all moths are airheads   its a loss to the
trade   im going to miss the little worm   tell you what suppose i
write you a poem myself in the contemporary manner   are you ready

lions roam the forest unfettered
the falcon soars   free as unconquered air
but i am trapped   in the body of a bug
my real name is lepisma saccarisma
though the unfeeling call me silverfish
ah god   what is the meaning of life interrogation point
shall i never transmigrate   into a form with dignity
and grace   worthy of a poet interrogation point

"Not falcons again," I said. "What's with you poets that you're so
hooked on lions and falcons?"

theyre symbols [wrote the silverfish] dont you know anything about
poetry interrogation point   ha ha   just the current poetic cliches

"Well, I sort of like 'free as unfettered air'," I admitted. "Is that
original?"

dont be silly another cliche   i just put that in for the wasp
but the two first lines dont read so badly   i mean theyre garbage
lions dont live in forests they live on the veldt   but the fact is
try as i may   i cant write as badly as yer average phoney poet
look out worm   here comes that goddamn cat again

They both disappeared, refusing flatly to continue the work, although my cat wouldn't dream of eating them. He won't even eat cat
food, unless he thinks the dog might like it. However, as neither dog
nor cat has ambitions as literary critics, this ends our study of contemporary poetry.

I will merely add that poetry started out with a song quality, or as
recitative, but since it has become an essentially written form, that
earlier function has been taken over by the music biz, in which
words are of secondary importance. As previously discussed, song
writers have never accepted the principle of poetic discipline: the
one-word or three-word song is increasing in frequency. And self-
styled poets, abjuring rhyme, rhythm, and scansion, are simply writ-

ing prose, although they'll never admit it. I once accused a student-poet of writing prose, and he replied that he couldn't be: he didn't even know what they were.

T. S. Eliot thought that poetry *had* to become more difficult, that meaning had to be wrenched . . . . whereas a Canadian poet, bill bissett, could write "a warm place to shit" all over a wall, and be taken seriously as both poet and painter. Critics wrote all sorts of pretentious stuff to prove that it "meant" something. The first eight lines of another bissett poem are,

were yu normal today did yu screw society

After the eighth inquiry, the poem continues:

did you blow cock eat cunt . . .
get lovers nuts and act on it do it all day
without cumming . . . did yu fuck the world today

And so on for a couple of pages. At least no one can accuse mr bissett of being difficult, although if he had read Cleanth Brooks ("The Well Wrought Urn") he might have had at least an intimation of the fact that suggestion is more effective than explicit pronouncement in poetry.

C. Day Lewis says ("The Poet's Way of Knowledge"),

Most poems which go wrong, go wrong through the poet's failure to extract the right theme, or extract it whole, from his subject matter. His activity during the initial stages of making a poem is equivalent to what [is called] "doubt" in scientific investigation: it is rigorous questioning of data – data which include the poem's original subject, the secondary subject – matter which is attracted into the field of the poem out of the poet's whole life experience, and the formal patterns into which he is beginning to arrange it. *This questioning is, for the poet as for the scientist, an arduous intellectual exercise.* (my italics)

There is no arduous intellectual effort manifested in the works of mr bissett, nor any rigorous questioning of data. His only metaphor is crude sexuality, which may be intended to shock. If so, it doesn't work, because it's been so dismally over-used. Or perhaps he has had no other life experience. Or perhaps he is just lazy and unimaginative.

If you don't accept me as an authority, let me quote again from that unassailable authority, T. S. Eliot. He says in "Tradition and the

Individual Talent" that ". . . the progress of an artist is a continual self-sacrifice, a continual extinction of the personality."

Contemporary poets will not accept this. They are obsessed with their personalities, although Freud (who may not have been a poet, but still knew a thing or two) said, in *A General Introduction to Psychoanalysis* that the artist must learn "how to lose that personal note which grates upon strange ears . . . how to modify [day-dreams] so that their origin in prohibited sources is not easily detected." This has never occurred to many of our would-be poets, with the result that the reader writhes with embarrassment on reading their work, which grates upon their ears. The following example is very slightly adapted from a published poem, but I have had thousands such submitted to me, with very slight variations. Substitute he for she, city for town, love for hate, and you practically cover the field. They have titles like "life" or "myself" or "pain". This one I'll call, let me think,

always alone

she was born in an ontario small town after the war
not a wanted child
her sister bullied her
she was good at sports but got no encouragement from her family
one dear friend took the place of family in her affections
she married to escape her home but was unhappy
   ran away decided to study art
cares deeply about literature painting and music
but cant get excited about politics
is concerned about the environment

And so on for three pages of self-indulgence.

I recommend for would-be poets another Eliot essay, "Reflections on *Vers Libre*," in which he states,

> *Vers libre* has not even the excuse of a polemic; it is a battle-cry of freedom, and there is no freedom in art . . . If *vers libre* is a genuine verse-form it will have a positive definition. And I can only define it in negatives: (1) absence of pattern, (2) absence of rhyme, (3) absence of metre.

He concludes, "there is only good verse, bad verse, and chaos."

All art requires discipline and craftsmanship. If you're too lazy to learn your craft, everything you do will be slovenly. It's a temptation, as Milton pointed out in "Lycidas"

Alas, what boots it with uncessant care
To tend the homely slighted shepherd's trade,
And strictly meditate the thankless Muse?
Were it not better done as others use,
To sport with Amaryllis in the shade,
Or with the tangles of Neæra's hair?

It's worth it, though. John Milton is still being quoted nearly four centuries later, but it is highly doubtful that anyone, ever, will feel strongly moved to quote *did yu screw society today*

Again, one cannot put all the blame on the new poets. A whole generation of students read, heard, and were taught nothing but free verse. They graduated from high school without having read a single one of the "monuments" of English literature: "Who is this guy Woodsworth you were talking about?" A course in poetry writing was given at post-secondary level by a teacher who didn't know what a sonnet was.

Perhaps the next generation will find new forms, new voices. There are straws in the wind; recently I've heard several songs with intelligible words. *Nil desperandum.* Perhaps some day a critic will have the courage to say, "The emperor has no clothes" or even "This stuff isn't poetry!"

CHAPTER

22

Coolspeak and Other In-Talk

The Sixties didn't really arrive in Canada until the Seventies. We had seen "Hair", and were conscious of the strange things that were happening to clothes and language and human relations, but it was all still rather remote and west-coast-oriented. The Beatles had become Britain's most valuable export commodity. In 1969, in Ontario at least, schools still had rigid dress-codes. Girls were not allowed to wear slacks to school, and boys were continually under surveillance lest they let their shirts hang out. "Get a haircut!" was constantly on the lips of vice-principals.

Then, suddenly, a whole generation disappeared under a huge wave of hair. Male faces were all but invisible: a pair of eyes just perceptible between burgeoning hair and unkempt beard. Tidiness became contemptible, and people appeared on the streets, in classes, everywhere, barefoot and in rags. By choice.

Hair was a matter of the utmost urgency. Families broke up over it. Instead of the stereotypical undergraduate (clean-shaven, short on back and sides, outré sports shirts and loud jackets? – I've forgotten what the stereotype undergraduate looked like), the corridors were thronged with Jesus Christ look-alikes, deep in earnest discussion with William Ewart Gladstones and Walt Whitmans.

It was, at first, a revolution, a rebellion against materialism. It was also inextricably involved with the drug culture, and a kind of unfocused mysticism. The college where I taught was overhung with an almost palpable cloud of marijuana smoke. The most successful courses of study in this college were in visual arts and non-print media. The written word was held in very low esteem.

"Are you one of those teachers who want people to read *books?*" a graphic arts student asked me, apprehensively. How she said that word "books"! – as if I had been urging them to contract leprosy. Some extraordinary things happened to language in the Cool decade. Apart from the explosion of four-letter words, a strange new underground tongue emerged, strongly influenced by jazz and pop music, especially the Beatles, and by the theories of Marshall McLuhan, who was enormously interested in the phenomenon of Cool. He was accused of inventing it, but he didn't: he merely observed and documented it.

This was of course not the first such phenomenon; every age produces its In-talk and vogue words. We can tell from Mercutio's speech in *Romeo and Juliet* that "very" was once the affectation of a particular set:

> The pox of such anticks, lisping, affecting fantasticoes; these new tuners of accents! "By Jesu, a very good blade! – a very tall man! – a very good whore!" – Why is not this a lamentable thing . . . that we should be thus afflicted with these strange flies, these fashion-mongers, these *pardonnez-moys*, who stand so much on the new form, that they cannot sit at ease on the old bench! Oh, their *bons*, their *bons!*(Act 2, sc. 4)

A denunciation of French Classy, as well.

Skipping a few centuries, we find the Pre-Raphaelites developing a specialized In-talk, which apparently aroused a good deal of criticism in its day, particularly for its habit of describing girls as "stunners" and "smashers", which was considered disrespectful to ladies, though most of us wouldn't mind being so described. Painters and poets, they were as glamorous to the outsider as musicians are in the contemporary world. They were equally snobbish with amateurs.

The first such specialized discourse that I can remember was the service talk of the Second World War. I wasn't part of it, but I overheard it from my elders, and yearned to be able to join in, but didn't dare. It was the mark of the insider, of the in-group, specifically designed to exclude the outsider. Most of it originated with the Royal Air Force.

"This character [or joker] pranged his kite." Tr.: This person crashed his plane. A character or joker was someone the speaker didn't know personally; joker often had a faintly derogatory suggestion, although it had nothing to do with making jokes.

Nice girls were, for no perceptible reason, "wittle characters". A bad girl, or one the speaker didn't like, was a "haggish-baggish". Boring conversation, usually by non-members of the club, was natter, or yacketty-yack. In almost none of the specialized languages does anyone die: in service speech you bought it, or *had* it, strongly accented. When wives or girl-friends protested against shop-talk, the men didn't stop talking – they promised to close the hangar doors. (But never did.)

After the war, new patois emerged, strongly influenced by music, especially jazz, which has always had its own cryptic private diction. Some of the words had probably been in use among jazz musicians as long ago as the Twenties, and in the Thirties (the age of Swing, when hot music was what we later described as cool). Hip, beat, cat, and dig have long been in the vocabulary of musicians, although with unconventional meanings; they emerged into general use in the Sixties. Hep, a variation of hip, and bop, shortened form of bebop (onomatopoeic, to suggest the beat) are difficult to date, other than 20th century, which isn't much help. Outsiders who tried to use in-talk, hoping for acceptance, were regarded with contempt. Impostors who imitated the insiders' dress and life-style were snubbed. "Like, it ain't beat to be beat, man," was the judgement of Dizzy Gillespie.

The Sixties/Seventies (in its own terms) was something else. Most new languages are the creation and property of the young, but never has the generation gap been so marked as in that period. "Never trust anyone over thirty," said Jerry Rubin, who apparently thought that he had some magic recipe for stopping time for himself and his group, but time has betrayed him, making him bald and bulgy.

One of the really dreadful side-effects of the period was the tragedy of the middle-aged would-be hippy. Many professors, in spite of grey hair and bulging waistlines, ardently identified with youth. They threw off their three-piece suits, their shabby corduroy jackets and flannels, and squeezed themselves into blue jeans. They let their hair grow. They sported sideburns (or boards). Long hair can look attractive on the young (if it's clean, which it frequently isn't) but it is not becoming to the senior citizen. One middle-aged gent of my acquaintance truly believed he was indistinguishable from his students: cool city, man. It was exquisitely embarrassing to hear him try to shed his normal scholarly vocabulary and adopt the jargon: "Hey, far out. Great threads, man." One day he told me something really heavy – a cool chick had been ripped off by someone wigged out on acid. He gave up conversation for rapping. He dug everything. Eventually he blew his gig, split from Academia, grooved into a commune of some sort, and hasn't been seen since. The sad thing was that he was despised by the students for whom he felt such empathy.

They had no compunction about bleeding him for money, and they made cruel fun of him. There was no crime like being old (i.e., over thirty) but it was compounded if the offender pretended to be young, and hoped for acceptance. The role assigned to elders was that of the oppressor; their sympathy wasn't wanted. They were required to be incapable of understanding, and to be chronically shocked. The cool generation impoverished the language as no previous rebellion has done. They refused to read, they resisted all disciplines, artistic or otherwise. Their vocabularies, apart from the easily exhausted hip-talk and four-letter words, were hopelessly limited. (Among the musicians where the language originated, it no doubt had a great deal of vitality and authenticity, but this gets lost when it is secondhand and simply imitative.)

One of the apostles of Cool was Bob Dylan, a performer whose popularity always baffled me. He can't play the guitar, and he can't sing. In fact, he must be one of the worst singers in human history. One of my students, a dedicated Dylan fan, conceded that he couldn't sing or play, but insisted that his importance lay in the poetry: he really *said* it for the hip generation. I had read an article about Dylan which claimed he had started out hoping to inherit the mantle of Elvis Presley, who was despised among the cool and hip for his commercialism and popularity. However, the mantle of Elvis was utterly inaccessible to Dylan; Elvis, for all his weaknesses, had a good voice, and Dylan's is dreadful. He therefore identified with Cool and has since been canonized (in *The Catalogue of Cool*) as a hipster saint.

I can't speak authentically of Dylan's poetry, because I can't stand listening to him, but his song "Lay, lady, lay" offends (as previously discussed) against grammatical rules. Now song-writing conventions are different from those of other poetry, and one doesn't demand grammar. But "Lay, lady" – ugh! – is a pretentious attempt at songwriting. It thinks it's high class. It stinks. It's Songrite Classy. Fats Waller isn't grammatical in "Don't Like You Cause Your Feets Too Big", but I wouldn't dream of tampering with one sacred syllable: it's a masterpiece. "Yo' pedal extremities is really obnox-i-ous" still makes me writhe with pleasure.

My Dylan-fan student insisted that his work was highly intellectual – one of his songs mentioned James Joyce! That's all it was, a mention. Not a very great intellectual achievement: anyone can pick up a name and use it with no point or relevance. The following verse was pressed on me as an example of "meaningful poetry".

> Now the roving gambler he was very bored
> Trying to create a next world war
> He found a promoter who nearly fell off the floor
> He said, "I've never engaged in this kind of thing before."

This kind of sloppy writing and thinking hasn't one thing to recommend it. It says nothing. It doesn't scan. Look at the rhyme – no plan, no discipline, no control. Any genuine poet would be ashamed of such poor craftsmanship.

"He's against war!" explained my student.

Oh, how original! What a slovenly way of saying so. Let's do a little analysis on this meaningful poem.

Who is this roving gambler, what does he represent? If we have a "next world war" it will be the work of such powers as the Pentagon, and the military-industrial complex, which are far from being roving gamblers. Please don't tell me that it's a covert reference to someone like Ronald Reagan or George Bush, neither of whom could be described in any sense as "a roving gambler". How do you "create" a war? And while starting wars is abominable and murderous, it could never be classified as boring. Who is this promoter? Promoter of what? How could he, or anyone else, fall off a floor? He might fall down on the floor, or he might fall off a cliff, but you *can't* fall off a floor. This isn't a poem, it's a piece of slovenly fakery, without one redeeming feature. How it could impose on anyone is incomprehensible. Such an imposition could only happen to people who have no sensitivity to words, no capacity for analysis or criticism.

No self-respecting craftsman could endure to have his name associated with writing like Dylan's "poem". He/she would die of shame at the thought. "Artists are by nature versatile and precise," observed Evelyn Waugh. "They only repine when involved with the monotonous and the makeshift." There is nothing precise in Dylan's writing, but there is a great deal of the makeshift.

Slovenly language makes it easier to have slovenly thoughts. It makes you vulnerable to the machinations of the worst sort of charlatans and swindlers. It makes you incapable of recognizing a put-on.

The world of cool and hip gradually disappeared. Dylan, with a typical lack of integrity, jumped on the next bandwagon and became a born-again Christian. I believe he has since fallen off that one, too, but I must admit I haven't followed his career.

The rebellion against materialism died ignominiously, capitulating to the ethic of the two-car garage and the four-bathroom house. The communes collapsed. Suddenly the college was full of girls with nylon hose, high heels and fancy hair-dos. The boys wore suits and ties. The hippies vanished; the yuppies appeared.

The cool generation spent most of its time listening to records, whose grooves gave them one of their most important words. To groove, or be groovy, was an eminently desirable state. (It's still used, to express favour, but now that the compact disc has replaced the grooves of the L.P., its meaning has been lost.) Music was a religion to the hippies, the band members their gods. When John Lennon was murdered, the hippies and ex-hippies felt as if the world had come to an end. He was a Christ-figure to them.

Their generation apprehended the world through music, films, and television, which were of extraordinary importance to them. I was once asked to change the date of an examination because several people couldn't be in class that day: there was to be a crucial episode of "General Hospital" which they absolutely couldn't miss. (This was in the prehistoric era before the VCR was a household staple.)

Many of them were close to illiteracy as far as written language was concerned, although they all seemed able to read and write just enough to pass a driver's test. (Which doesn't say much for drivers' tests.) For many of them, however, cars were not important, and this was interesting if one recalls the car-obsessions of the Fifties and

Eighties. The hippies were not "into" cars, except for essential transportation, and for long-distance travel they preferred to hitch-hike. They thumbed millions of miles. I remember being surprised when a commune-dwelling acquaintance announced (or seemed to be announcing), "We're going to get us a car," as they had never had the smallest interest in cars previously. They still didn't; I had misunderstood her hip mumble. She had really said, "We're going to get a sitar." They spent their money on records, musical instruments, concerts, and drugs – usually pot, although most of them experimented with hard drugs occasionally. Like the wartime flyers with planes, and the Eskimos with snow, the hippies had hundreds of words for marijuana.

A few of them were articulate in speech, if not in the written word, but most of them had great difficulty in expressing any ideas, falling back on words and set phrases for all occasions: "heavy, far out, cool," supplemented abundantly by "like" and "y'know".

Nevertheless, there was something appealing about the Cool Generation. They were usually stoned to the eyeballs, and capable of expressing only the most basic ideas, but they had an innocence and honesty that made them more appealing than their slick yuppy successors. Many of them were genuinely non-materialistic; they were gentle and non-sexist. They deplored "head-trips", or manipulation.

An earlier group of rebels, the Angry Young Men, were vicious and abusive toward women – see *Look Back in Anger, The Ginger Man*, the Amis *œuvre*.

The post-hippy period has been marked by extreme and overt violence against women. Whether theirs was a genuine philosophic position, or simply lethargy resulting from the ingestion of huge quantities of pot, the Cool generation had an attractive mildness. They were often inefficient and passive, but in an age of wife-beaters, rapists, and abusers, one can't but feel nostalgia for the days of the dreamy hippies, who did their tripping on pot rather than on power.

The yuppies were arrogant, over-confident, and mouthy. They poured in their thousands into the colleges, to study advertising, journalism, business, and engineering. They were more articulate than the hippies, but they still couldn't spell, or write a sentence. I warned one young man who was heading for a career in sales that his atrocious spelling would be a handicap in business. He laughed, explaining loftily that he would have a secretary to look after that stuff.

"What makes you think your secretary will know how to spell?" asked the mean old teacher, for the spelling of the young ladies in Secretarial Studies was as execrable as his own. But perhaps he was right. If we're going to live in a world where no one can spell, who's going to criticize another person's bad spelling? Or even recognize it when it appears?

Oddly enough, after the hippies disappeared, a nostalgic cult of pseudo-, or ersatz-Cool, appeared. Its members tried to speak the language, and professed hero-worship for some of the same musicians. *The Catalog of Cool*, published in 1982, proclaims its spurious quality on every page. It was obsessed, for heaven's sake, with *clothes*, whereas the genuinely Cool wore rags. Photos of allegedly cool heroes show clean-shaven young men with short hair and expensive "threads". They wear ties, something no hippy dreamed of possessing. They are competitive and ostentatious and crazy about cars. However, they do have one thing in common with the genuinely cool cats: they're very poor at verbalizing. *The Catalog of Cool* includes a dictionary of hip talk, consisting of fifty-nine words. Although it was compiled a comparatively short time ago, none of the vocabulary – except a few words like cool, inherited from the genuinely hip – has survived. Few of the terms cited in the dictionary had any real currency; they are laborious fakes. For example:

> *Betty's world:* Referring to any geopolitical event occurring during the reign of Elizabeth I (1558-1603).
> *Big Deuce:* World War II.
> *bourbon:* Lost in space, a general state of fuzzy-mindedness
> *to do it like Mommy:* To come on domestic in a big way.
> *Leo-time:* August
> *Mister Ed:* An unimpeachable inside source.

They may profess to be Cool, but they're about as convincing as twentieth-century Druids.

I have tried to keep up with In-language trends since the days of the hippies, but nothing as revolutionary as Cool-speak has emerged. Currently my sources are two juvenile family members, Ben and Jake, aged ten and six respectively. For some time, Ben's discourse was liberally decorated with references to "cool dudes", and the only permissible terms of approval were "awesome" and "radical" – later reduced to "rad". Once these terms filtered down to Jake's age group, the elder sophisticates abandoned them: kid stuff. "Eeeclectic!" is currently used with no connection whatsoever to the meaning of the word.

"Hey, this is really eeeclectic!" said Ben, one sunny day when we were skating on a frozen pond.

What did he mean by eclectic? Well – great. Neat. Wow. Rad. Cool, even.

He had learned it from watching the Ninja Turtles.

The roots of the latest coolspeak, it appears, are in the specialized demotic speech of surfing, just as the idiosyncratic jive talk of of earlier periods came from the private language of jazz musicians.

A dictionary of surfing terms *The Surfin'ary* by Trevor Calle, attempts to document them; it claims that "Surfspeak" originated with ancient surfing Hawaiians, although its roots are clearly English, except possibly for "Cowabunga!", the triumphant cry of the surfer riding a big wave, or smoker. (Or honker, or dozens of others. Wave vocabulary for the surfers, like snow-vocabulary for Inuits, is full of nuances and specializations.)

Parasitism by non-initiates produces contempt among the In (like, it's not beat to be beat, man) and many words lose their cachet when they are appropriated by outsiders. There are some hardy perennials that go back as far as the Thirties: cool, hot, groovy, and the ubiquitous and meaningless interpolation, *like, you know.* Current manifestation: "Like, Hi."

I'm not personally acquainted with the Valley Girls phenomenon, but a friend tells me that these poachers on surfing language are rich *RICH* California girls, who lust after the bleached blonde, dark tanned surfers, and try to appropriate their vocabulary. "Like, you know, he's to die for. Awesome, totally rad."

Although the specialized language is often discarded by the In group once it has drifted into general usage, and new words have to be found to exclude the outside world, it has its effect on language in general, and in some cases it may sorta like, y'know, heavily enrich our vocabularies, bro.

The Ninja Turtles and other poachers have appropriated the inspeak, shouting "Cowabunga!"

Specialized languages appear – and disappear – like summer storms. A friend has just sent me an article by Peter Goddard, from the Toronto *Star*, on Lower Rosedale Logo Talk – "the emerging form of communication of the 1990s". It seems to be based on brand-names, and is of great value within the group in evaluating class levels, the way an Oxbridge accent once immediately established a speaker as being "one of Ours", whereas a Lancashire dialect put him beyond the pale forever.

Now [says Goddard] if you say "Birkenstock" rather than the diminutive "Birks",

> you reveal yourself to be an *arriviste* of the worst sort and quite unsuitable for membership in the RCYC, BSS, the B and R, TSE or UCC. See?

Good God, it all boils down to snobbery, of the most vulgar kind, which in the starry-eyed Sixties we believed we had outgrown. Good God, it all boils down to snobbery!

CHAPTER

23

Lying Language

Yet another category of language abuse might be described as "mealymouthisms". These aren't exactly euphemisms, but they have the effect of making something offensive sound a lot milder than it really is. Many of these were invented by and for the film and TV industries, so that they can sell something offensive as therapeutic. The same system is used by government for intolerable economic policies.

Adult really means Dirty. Usually involves two or more naked men and women rolling around in bed (or on a beach, in a field, *n'importe*). This, as Woody Allen and Monty Python have demonstrated, can be ludicrous rather than aphrodisiac ("Bananas," the Sex Education Class). The intention, however, is to act as a stimulant to a drooly form of sexual excitement. Its appeal is to sufferers from voyeurism.

Erotic: Dirty. Two or more naked men rolling around in bed together; OR two or more naked women rolling around in bed together; OR combinations of both.

Realism: Dirty. Incest, rape, sodomy, child prostitution, sadomasochism, bestiality, battering, wounding, etc., but done with very serious facial expressions suggesting it is not enjoyable but has social relevance. Includes as much stark nakedness as is feasible in the Canadian climate.

Unacceptable: Not used in the entertainment world but occurs frequently in news, in all forms of media. It means outrageous, criminal, inexcusable. "Abuse of young children by priests and brothers is unacceptable." Dramatized for the entertainment world, it becomes

Starkly realistic: Dirty. Priests and brothers, stark naked under their robes, inappropriately abusing stark naked young children. A favourite with contemporary film-makers, always done with severe facial expressions and allegedly high moral intent.

Physical/Very physical: Used by sportswriters of games and athletes, especially hockey players. "He plays a very physical game." What they really mean is that he's violent, sometimes maiming and crippling his opponents on camera, while thousands cheer.

A fruitful source of mealymouthisms is, of course, government.

Direct Public Ownership: This comes from Michael Wilson's 1991 budget, with its announcement of the sale of Petro-Canada to private investors or speculators. Mr. Wilson spoke of turning over a company that belongs to the taxpayers to "direct public ownership" that is, taking it *out of* public ownership and handing it over to private interests for exploitation, at the taxpayers' expense. This is a nice example of using words to suggest exactly the opposite of what they really mean.

Inappropriate: Mealymouthism for dishonest, crooked, sneaky. "The politician's misappropriation of funds was inappropriate."

Two interesting new words emerged on the political scene in the 1980s: *Thatcherism* and *Reaganomics.* (May we now add *Mulronomics?*) All are based on the monetarist theories of Milton Friedman, according to which

> management of the country's economy, espec. in the achievement
> of a reduced rate of inflation, by control of the money supply . . .
> requires cutting of govt. spending [and] is regarded as in the short-
> term eliminating waste and in the long term *as a means of returning*
> *to the private sector as large a proportion of the economy as possible*
> *in order to attain greater efficiency.* (Italics mine).

Hutchinson's Encyclopedia, which provides this definition, praises Mrs. Thatcher's success in reducing inflation, while admitting that her policies created unanticipated increases in unemployment. But other definitions give the word a quite different meaning.

According to William Pfaff, international affairs columnist, writing in the Toronto *Star,* Thatcherism is a hard doctrine of pitiless privatization, submitting [everything] to the marketplace: planes, trains, water, electricity, health, art, entertainment, education, scientific research, the nation's future itself . . . Hordes of teenage beggars swarm all over London, and cardboard shanty towns have sprung up because of the housing shortage.

Noam Chomsky, Institute Professor of Linguistics and Philosophy at Massachusetts Institute of Technology, defined Reaganomics abroad as "Large-scale subversion and international terrorism." At home, it was

a systematic transfer of resources to the rich, partial dismantling of the limited welfare system, an attack on unions and real wages, and expansion of public subsidy for high-technology industry through the Pentagon . . . *Deterring Democracy*, p. 81.

That's the democratic way to eliminate waste and achieve efficiency?

It is interesting that George Bush once defined Reaganomics as "voodoo economics." However, he soon saw the light – indeed, a thousand points of light – and embarked on a program which followed Reaganomic principles of making the rich still richer, in the interest of turning America into a kinder, gentler nation.

Mulronomics: has as yet no accepted definition, possibly because I just this minute invented the word. However, we know that it also embraces the Friedman monetarism, and devotedly follows Thatcher Reagan-Bush models.

Mulronomics produced what Michael Wilson called *a budget of opportunity . . . that challenges Canadians by rewarding success, not subsidizing effort*. But another definition of Mulronomics is *Reverse Robin-Hoodism*, by which the government robs the poor to subsidize the rich who, according to tax lawyer Neil Brooks, "made money like bandits . . . while ordinary people lost ground."

The American Way: We're all familiar, through films and advertisements, with the prototypical image of that white house on Elm Street, with roses growing on the white picket fence and honeysuckle twinin' round the porch. Although in the real world practically no one lives here, in the myth it's inhabited by Dick, Jane, Spot, Fluff, Mummy and Daddy. Or, alternatively, Ozzie and Harriett and the boys. Here no one sleeps on the streets, or lives by prostitution and crime. In the real world many people sleep on the street, but as Ronald Reagan explained, they prefer sleeping outdoors.

The Canadian Way is exactly the same, only one-tenth the size, and with snow, the RCMP, and a few picturesque francophone peasants. Perhaps fewer guns, but we're catching up.

The U.S. sees itself as "the Mother Teresa of nations, always educating, wiping out disease, and saving humanity from fascism, communism, and war itself," according to Richard Barnet, in *The Rockets' Red Glare*.

In other parts of the world, where "Yankee Go Home" signs proliferate, little resemblance is perceived between Uncle Sam and Mother Teresa. Same package, different labels.

Democracy is inalienably associated with the American/Canadian Way. In a democracy, everyone lives in that white house with the picket fence, etc. Any child born in the U.S. or Canada may grow up to become President or Prime Minister. In actual practice, no one has ever held either office except a white male, usually a millionaire, unless he is (like Ronald Reagan) merely a front and a mouthpiece for millionaires.

You see how it works: governments say one thing, and by a kind of verbal legerdemain, turn it into its opposite. The media, which are owned by the élite establishment, fail to expose the sinister practices behind the inspiring language. (Sometimes they simply don't know what's going on, any more than the rest of us.) Most of us spend our lives in a state of helpless bafflement, unable to understand what's happening, why we are poor and helpless, or what forces are manipulating us.

The only answer is to educate ourselves. Learn to recognize the subtle lies by which our governments deceive and delude us. Some of the books I've mentioned here are great eye-openers, and even if you can't afford to buy books, you can get them from the library. Read Linda McQuaig, Maude Barlow, and Noam Chomsky for brilliant insights into the workings of lying language.

24

Patriotism and Propaganda

"**P**atriotism is the last refuge of a scoundrel," Samuel Johnson announced one night ("in a strong determined tone"), startling the company. Boswell adds a cautious qualification: "He did not mean a real and generous love of country, but that pretended patriotism which so many, in all ages and countries, have made a cloak for self-interest. I maintained that certainly all patriots were not scoundrels." But when he tried to prove his case, Johnson soon had him on the ropes.

In spite of the Great Lexicographer's famous apophthegm (dat's a good woid, but it's Boswell's, not mine), patriotism is still esteemed as a virtue. Perhaps we should spend a little time examining it, and its relationship to propaganda.

It is, as Johnson pointed out, frequently used as a disguise, or cloak, for villainy. When politicians orate about love of country, their deep unwavering patriotism – watch them! It's usually a cover for something expensive and destructive. No one has preached more eloquently about patriotism than our present Prime Minister; he almost brings tears to his own eyes when he declaims his devotion to Canada, precisely when he is most busily selling her down the river.

Patriotism has always been exploited for propaganda purposes. If people's emotions are sufficiently aroused, and their critical intelligence insufficiently developed, they can be persuaded to swallow almost anything. Judgement is destroyed by a rush of patriotism to the head.

Propaganda is not a new invention; it's probably been around for as long as governments have wanted to hoodwink the public by appeals to their love of country. Such appeals have great power in the United States, where the citizenry can be roused to jingoistic fury by phrases like "My country right or wrong", or "Better dead than Red". All critical judgement is suspended, all humane instincts suppressed, if the public can be persuaded that their homeland is in danger. Force and violence are the only recourses, even though the threats come from such improbable sources as Grenada or Nicaragua.

One of the interesting techniques employed in propaganda is the use of labels. The same event or practice gets a favourable label if We do it, an unfavourable label if They do it. In passing, *We* are always good, and *They* are always bad, for starters – even though both sides are behaving with equal iniquity.

For example: when our side builds up huge armaments, that is *defence*. When someone we don't like does the same thing, that is *aggression*. When innocent civilians are killed by our bombs, that is *incontinent ordnance* or *collateral damage*; if by their bombs, it's a *vicious atrocity*. When we marshall huge displays of armaments, send fleets of aircraft to fly right to the enemy's borders, or flotillas of battleships to prowl just outside their ports, it is a *show of strength*, undertaken to convince aggressors that we're too strong to be trifled with. If they do this, it is *attempted intimidation*, or *provocation*.

A few others from the Gulf War: *Air defence assets* sound innocuous, but in fact, they're bombs. The 200 daily air sorties were *protective reaction strikes*, or *pre-emptive counter attacks*, a nice oxymoron meaning one attacks the enemy first, thus pre-empting his attack, and making a counter-attack unnecessary. This is useful for when someone says, "You started it!" An interesting one is "friendly fire", used when soldiers are killed by their own side. With friends like that . . .

Espionage is an essential activity for our side; it's also known as surveillance, intelligence, or counter-intelligence. When They do it, it's *spying*, and counter-intelligence is *betrayal* or even *treason*.

A fine illustration of labelling technique occurred during the Gulf War, when an oil slick on the gulf gained world-wide attention. It was at one time "a small slick" and at others "the world's largest oil spill". This was explained in a modest little story in the Toronto *Star* (20 February, 1991, p. A15):

> Western military officers have said American attacks on Iraqi tankers off Kuwait early in the war caused another spill and the U.S.

shelling of coastal installations contributed to it. At the time, U.S. military officials said a "small slick" resulted from attacks on a tanker they claimed was involved in reconnaissance on the coalition armada in the gulf . . . Pictures of the slick at the border of the town of Khafji gained world-wide attention and reports of the world's largest oil spill played an important role in uniting international opinion against Iraq.

While *we* are always good, and *they* are always evil, *their* identity tends to shift bewilderingly. In 1991, Saddam Hussein became the world's most evil individual – "Satan Incarnate", according to one patriot. But in 1979 he had been a splendid fellow – "A man you could do business with". Is there any higher praise?

I've already touched on the curious linguistics of *democracy* (= good, = freedom) and *communism* (= evil, = slave state). A study of these two words in contemporary propaganda and journalism could be a life's work. Generally, democracy is believed to be government of the people, by the people, and for the people.

Henry Kissinger gave it a new twist when the public became restive against the huge expenditures on nuclear arms, and there was the threat of a "peace offensive" from the Soviets. Kissinger was concerned that if the public ceased to fear a real nuclear threat, " . . . popular support for the maintenance of forces could fade." If this disaster should occur, he suggested modestly, " . . . governments might feel themselves compelled to provide for deterrence *without the consent of the governed*." – Barnet, p. 390, (my italics).

The consent of the governed is supposed to be indispensable for democracy. What is the word for a government which imposes its will without that consent? Words like tyranny and fascism come to mind.

Perhaps the most famous propaganda technique is the Big Lie, made famous by Hitler and Goebbels. Tell a lie so outrageous that people won't know how to analyse or criticize it. I saw this demonstrated in the most exquisitely ironic way in an anti-choice protest, where a huge banner proclaimed, "Hitler was pro-choice, too!" This was a marvellous illustration of Hitler's own methods, because it was an absolute lie.

Hitler was violently anti-choice. Abortion was punishable by death in Nazi Germany, the only such case known to history. Women were traitors if they didn't bear good Aryan children to carry on the priceless genes. Non-Aryan women, however, were sometimes forced to have abortions. No choice at all. That's the great strength of propaganda – it doesn't allow itself to be hampered by trifles like facts, or truth.

Ronald Reagan, though he often seemed far from brilliant, was a faithful practitioner of this technique. He once told a trusting nation that the Russian language had no word for "freedom". It's a fairly silly lie, because it can easily be checked; but that's the point. People *don't* check. The stupider among us accept such statements as gospel, and pass them on as fact. The Russian word for freedom is *svoboda*.

Disinformation is a Reagan-period coining for lying. When Oliver North admitted – almost bragged – that he had lied to Congress, lying took on a new respectability – because boy-hero Ollie lied out of patriotism. It was his great love for his country that prompted clean-cut Ollie to make deals with Iran, set up with General Noriega methods to smuggle arms into San Salvador, and supply yet more arms to the Contras. General Noriega was okay in those days; he became evil when the Americans wanted an excuse for invading Panama. The 1999 date for expiry of American control of the canal was coming near, and it became essential to find a scapegoat. Noriega was not an admirable character, but they'd been working with him for years; he'd been praised for his good work in controlling the drug trade, and lavishly rewarded. Once a *co-operative ally*, he suddenly became *an odious dictator*.

Oliver North made lying respectable and patriotic, but the word still had rather disreputable associations. It was therefore promoted to, or disguised as, *disinformation*. One may still feel a certain degree of guilt, or at least discomfort, about deliberately lying, whereas *conveying disinformation* has a patriotic tinge: its ostensible purpose is to mislead the enemy. Its real purpose may be to deceive Congress, as well as one's friends and countrymen, but that is never admitted. In any case, it's done *for our own good*, because ordinary voters can't possibly understand the complexities of international affairs, especially when there's a danger of war. And there's always a danger of war, if Ollie and his buddies can arrange it.

Historically, it's been axiomatic that Peace = Good. We good guys are always in favor of peace, while They are out to start a war. This took a curious twist during the Cold War, however, when "defence" came to be equated with big profits, which were threatened whenever we were menaced by Soviet peace offensives, producing "The Unsettling Specter of Peace" headline in the *Wall Street Journal*, and a series of "peace scares". Economists and militarists alike have shuddered at the dread sound of the "Peace Dividend", by which money would be spent on health and education and the environment instead of on nukes. It's a Strangelove world, in which we have learned to love the bomb.

Peace frequently means war. Ernie Regehr, in *Arms Canada*, (p. xiv) notes that all weapons are strictly for peaceful purposes.

> The U.S. Air Force . . . designates its fighter aircraft sales programs with the prefix 'peace'. Thus sales to Israel, Saudi Arabia, Egypt, and Japan are code-named 'Peace Fox', 'Peace Sun', 'Peace Arrow', 'Peace Marble', and 'Peace Eagle'.

A lethal missile is "The Peacekeeper."

Chemical Warfare is never practised by the United States or Canada, although both of those sainted nations manufacture chemical weapons, and the U.S. devastated thousands of acres in Vietnam and Cambodia with Agent Orange. In 1968, a nerve agent, VX, which kills by asphyxiation, was accidentally released in Utah, causing the death of 6000 sheep. Their death was blamed (at least for awhile) on extra-terrestrials; the super-market tabloids rejoiced that at last we had proof positive of the existence of hostile aliens! The Army at first maintained a demure silence, then denied responsibility, but was ultimately forced to admit guilt, and to compensate angry farmers, who didn't buy the space alien story. Thomas Whiteside, in a two-part article called "The Yellow-Rain Complex", gives a hair-raising account of America's secret passion for biological and chemical weapons. (*The New Yorker*, Feb. 11 and 19, 1991). He also describes their furious condemnation of such devices in the hands of regimes of whom they disapprove, and their faking of evidence for its use by the Bad Guys.

Just in passing, Chomsky unearthed some blood-chilling quotations in this connection, one from my former hero, Winston Churchill, who complained about "this squeamishness about using gas. I am strongly in favour of using poisoned gas against uncivilized tribes . . ." By arbitrarily labelling human beings as "uncivilized tribes", Churchill makes the use of poison gas legitimate. The same technique was used by Norman Podhoretz, who rejoiced (apropos of the invasion of Grenada) that Americans had finally overcome their "sickly inhibitions about the use of force." The use of force is usually associated with bullies and brutes, but the "sickly" label makes it feeble and unmanly to oppose violence. For admirers of Rambo and John Wayne, such language is a call to arms. One of the chief uses of propaganda is to trigger emotional reactions that will stampede the gullible into war.

Speaking of heroes (and ex-heroes), I came across a splendid new word, *heroized*, coined by Richard Darman, Ronald Reagan's adviser on re-election. He planned a campaign

> . . . to paint RR as the personification of all that is right with, or heroized by, America . . . A vote against Reagan is . . . a vote against a mythic AMERICA." – (Barnet, p. 374)

Genocide and Terrorism These activities are strictly monopolized by regimes of whom the U.S. disapproves. When the U.S. or its friends do the same thing, it's in defence of democracy, or the American Way. Thus legitimately elected socialist regimes in Nicaragua and Chile were condemned as Marxist-Leninism, or creeping socialism, or communist infiltration, which are by definition evil, and so warrant intervention and even invasion. This can be easily achieved by the Orwellian device of double-think, while supporting murderous generals in Argentina, Korea, the Philippines, and Brazil.

Perhaps the most conspicuous example of language perversion occurred when a Vietnamese village had to be destroyed "in order to save it."

I very nearly forgot one of the most conspicuous examples of lying language. *Security*, or *national security*, has come to mean the building and accumulating of enormous quantities of weapons so lethally destructive that they cannot be used without jeopardizing life on the planet. Their manufacture is environmentally destructive; their storage is dangerous and expensive; even if we have an attack of sanity and decide to destroy them, that process is risky and expensive. But it's nice to have security, isn't it?

Propaganda is the worst of language abuses. Slovenly or deliberately distorted language makes it easier for us to have slovenly thoughts, to accept the prettified words without considering their real purpose. Slovenly thinking makes possible the outrages (human, economic, and environmental) that we have witnessed too often in the names of freedom, democracy, and patriotism.

25

Conclusion

A melancholy development of the Sixties decade, which has contributed materially to the degradation of language, was a belief that good grammar, correct pronunciation, precision in the use of words all that gave English its elegance and clarity – were no longer important. They were pedantries, symptoms of snobbery and obsolete thinking.

What mattered – the only thing that mattered – was *feelings*. The half-stoned inarticulate mumbling, "Like, y'know, it was like, far out, I mean, like real heavy, okay?" was believed to be making a signifi-cant statement. Somehow this fuzzy stuff was attributed to the theo-ries of Marshall McLuhan – not because he was guilty of it, but be-cause he saw it coming, and warned us. Superficially read by incompetent readers, McLuhan was constantly cited as authorizing and validating Coolspeak. Slovenly language makes it easy to have foolish thoughts; it also makes for careless reading.

Whenever I protested, during my teaching career, against sloppy speech and writing, I was accused of "linear thinking". I've also been accused of trying to "freeze" the language in its present state, resist-ing all change, although this is a complete misrepresentation of my convictions. Language *must* change, and will whether we like it or not. I just don't want it to change for the worse. I want it to be elo-quent, flexible, versatile, and adaptable, but simple and easy to un-derstand.

Personally, I like slang, which often enriches our speech, and can give a nice casual tone. I don't like formal, pedantic speech or writing; my preference is for a conversational and personal style.

We all need to know how language works, and the only way to do this is to study grammar. Not for snobbish reasons, to sound "U" (for Upper Class), but simply in the interest of clarity and precision.

Unfortunately, many students rebel against such propositions. Why should they bother with the tedious stuff, they argue, if they can get a job in television journalism on the strength of a pretty face, even though they can't write a grammatical sentence and have never consulted a dictionary in their lives.

First, because none of us stays young and pretty forever, and we have to have some other qualifications once the wrinkles and bulges begin. (And they always do, eventually, difficult though it is for us to believe at twenty-one.) Second, because if you are going to work in a field that deals in words, you must learn to use your tools efficiently and correctly. Otherwise, you'll always be second-rate. Third, because you damned well have an obligation to your audience to provide a sound model. You're as reprehensible as the man calling himself a carpenter, who undertakes to build you a house when he doesn't know how to drive a nail. If you're setting a bad example for generations to come, you should lose your job, and I hope you do. So there!

(You'll note, in the last paragraph, that I didn't say firstly, secondly, thirdly, nor yet first of all, second of all, etc. The reason I didn't is that they are pointless. If a thing is first, it's by definition first of all. It begins to sound silly with "second of all" and gets progressively sillier the higher you go. "Eighty-third of all," for example. The addition of "ly" is the result of some dim idea that an adverb is needed in this construction, and so it is. But first, along with the rest of them, is both adverb and adjective, so that the "ly" is a waste of time and space.)

As I trust is now abundantly clear, I believe that the two major ailments afflicting language today are the Classy Syndrome, and ignorance of the fundamentals of grammar. Associated with these are such problems as ill-advised methods of teaching grammar, spelling, pronunciation, and failure to use a dictionary.

Grammar should be restored to the English curriculum at an early stage, so that it is absorbed almost by osmosis. (If it's taught properly, by a teacher who knows his/her stuff, grammar can be great fun. This is, of course, true of practically every subject.) But there's absolutely no use in having grammar taught by someone who isn't himself well-grounded in the subject, so that we have to start by educating teachers.

For some reason, perhaps a form of insanity, there is a persistent idea that reading should be taught by EITHER phonetics or by word-recognition. Wars have been fought, are still being fought, over this ridiculous idea. Obviously, in a language like English, WE NEED BOTH. Generations of kids have been sent out into the world unable to decipher a simple sentence because of a lunatic belief that it is wrong and wicked to teach a child to sound out a word.

Not just English teachers, but ALL teachers should be required to take a good, tough, sound, uncompromising course in grammar, with drills in spelling and pronunciation, so that they'll all be able to set a good example for their students, whether they're teaching art or geography or motor mechanics. They'll hate it, but they'll thank you for it later.

However, the work can't be confined to schools. We can teach good language practices until we're blue in the face, but if the kids go out of school and hear journalists and politicians and librarians saying "eck cetera" and "anyways, like I said", the efforts of the school will be undone. Everyone who works with words, and can influence the speech and writing patterns of the impressionable young, should be compelled to take the course. (It could be a summer course, or even several summer courses.)

Writers of all stripes, and their editors; secretaries and their bosses; politicians and their aides; librarians and everyone in the book and magazine and newspaper trade; everyone in radio and television and film and theatre; everyone in advertising – all of them need to understand how language works, and how to use it effectively.

The course I'm thinking of wouldn't teach anything fancy. No "creative writing", no criticism or literary studies. Just good clear communication. The less fancy the better. Then if people want to try something creative, they have the foundation for it. There is absolutely no sense in trying to be creative, or write imaginative literature, or anything of the sort, if you haven't mastered the fundamentals first. It's like insisting on playing a Beethoven Sonata before you've mastered Pop Goes the Weasel.

Truck drivers and plumbers and garage mechanics will argue that their business is not with words, and why don't I take a course in carburetors? Still, they have to read instruction manuals, and most of them are, or will sometime be, parents of children who must be taught to read and write and speak intelligibly. They should at least make an effort to set a good example, and be aware of the problem.

Most people hate grammar, because it has been badly taught. I was lucky in having several good teachers, and I actually enjoyed it. Almost everyone hated maths, because (except for arithmetic) they seemed to have no relation to life. They were simply exercises, devised to torture kids. They were supposed to "exercise your brain" as if the brain were some kind of muscle. If anyone had explained how they could be used in real-life situations, we might have enjoyed them. Most people detested geography, which was enforced memorization of lists: lists of rivers, of cities, of countries – tedious beyond belief. But geography, well taught, can be one of the most absorbing of studies. If you can see how it crosses with history, and history with literature, and all of these with the various fields of science, it becomes so exciting that you can hardly wait to get more of it. You want to learn *everything*.

T. H. White summed up beautifully the way education should function, in *The Sword in the Stone*:

"The best thing for disturbances of the spirit," said Merlyn . . . "is to learn. That is the only thing that never fails. You may grow old and trembling in your anatomies, you may lie awake at night listening to the disorder of your veins, you may miss your only love, you may see the world about you devastated by evil lunatics, or know your honour trampled in the sewers of baser minds. There is only one thing for it then – to learn. Learn why the world wags and what wags it. That is the only thing which the mind can never exhaust, never alienate, never be tortured by, never fear or distrust, and never dream of regretting. Learning is the thing for you. Look at what a lot of things there are to learn – pure science, the only purity there is. You can learn astronomy in a lifetime, natural history in three, literature in six. And then, after you have exhausted a milliard lifetimes in biology and medicine and theo-criticism and geography and history and economics – why, you can start to make a cartwheel out of the appropriate wood, or spend fifty years learning to begin to learn to beat your adversary at fencing. After that you can start again on mathematics, until it is time to learn to plough."

Bibliography

Auerbach, Erich. "Fortunato" in *Approaches to the Novel*, ed. Robert Scholes. San Francisco: Chandler, 1961.

Barnet, Richard J. *The Rockets' Red Glare*. N.Y.: Simon and Schuster, 1990.

Boswell, James. *The Life of Samuel Johnson*. N.Y.: Modern Library, n.d.

Bowler, Peter. *The Superior Person's Book of Words*. Boston: David R. Godine, 1987.

Carey, G. V. *Mind The Stop*. Harmondsworth: Penguin, 1958.

Chandler, Raymond. *Farewell, My Lovely* N.Y. Ballantine, 1940.

Chapman, Robert L., ed. *Roget's International Thesaurus*. New York: Thomas Y. Crowell, 1974.

Chomsky, Noam. *Deterring Democracy*. New York, Verso. 1991.

Empson, William. *Seven Types of Ambiguity*. Harmondsworth: Penguin, 1961.

Evans, Ivor H., ed. *Brewer's Dictionary of Phrase and Fable*. New York: Harper & Row, 1981.

Gup, Ted. "A Man You Could Do Business With" in *Time*, 11 March, 1991.

Kennedy, Margaret. *The Feast*. New York: Rhinehart. n.d.

Kerrod, Robin.(ed.) *The Concise Dictionary of Science*. New York: Arco Publishing, 1985.

Macaulay, Rose. *The Towers of Trebizond*. London: Collins, 1983.

marquis, don. *the lives and times of archy and mehitabel*. garden city: Doubleday, 1934.

McDowell, Jeanne. "Earth Day". *Time*, December, 1989.

Mitford, Nancy. *Noblesse Oblige*. Penguin Books, 1956.

Nurnberg, Maxwell. *Questions you always wanted to ask about English*. New York: Pocket Books, 1972.

Onions, C.T., J. Coulson, H. G. Fowler and William Little. *The Shorter Oxford Dictionary on Historical Principles*. Oxford: Clarendon Press, 1950.

Onions, C. T., G. W. S. Friedrichsen, and R. W. Burchfield. *The Oxford Dictionary of English Etymology*. Oxford, Clarendon Press, 1982.

Regehr, Ernie. *Arms Canada*. Toronto: James Lorimer & Co., 1987.

Sculatti, Gene. *The Catalog of Cool*. N.Y. Warner Books, 1982.

Sykes, J. B. ed. *The Concise Oxford Dictionary of Current English*. Oxford, Clarendon Press, 1976.

Strunk, William Jr. and E. B. White. *The Elements of Style*. New York: Macmillan, 1979.

Westlake, Donald C. *Dancing Aztecs*. Philadelphia: Lippincott, 1976.

— *Good Behaviour*. New York: TOR, 1988.

White, T. H. *The Sword in the Stone*. London: Collins, 1958.

Acknowledgments

To Carol Verdun of the *National Independent,* who read the first draft, caught errors, gave me good advice, and urged me to continue with it. I've also borrowed from her column, "Working with Words," in which she regularly collects and exposes Horrible Examples from the press.

A bow also to my editor, Shirley Knight Morris, whose interest in the subject and sensitivity to language have been invaluable.

Maxwell Nurnberg's delightful *Questions you always wanted to ask about English . . . but were afraid to raise your hand* made the teaching of English fun instead of torture, and I have leaned on it heavily in this book. Copyright, 1972, Pocket Books.

Fowler's *Modern English Usage,* Copyright, 1990, Oxford University Press, has been indispensable, as have the *Shorter Oxford Dictionary, The Concise Oxford, and The Oxford Dictionary of English Etymology.* I would be helpless without *Roget's International Thesaurus,* Copyright 1977, by Thomas Y. Crowell Company, inc.

Thanks to Donald Westlake for several choice bits, especially the one from *Dancing Aztecs,* Mysterious Press Books.

Lifelong debts to don marquis's archie the cockroach, and to T. H. White, whose recipe for disturbances of the spirit in *The Sword in the Stone* has always seemed to me the best advice any teacher ever gave to any student.

While many of my examples have come from within the CBC, I am still a dedicated listener/watcher, and could not live without the Corporation. May they never be sold out to the profit-makers!